THE
QUICK AND EASY
COLLEGE
COOKBOOK

300
HEALTHY, LOW-COST MEALS THAT FIT YOUR BUDGET AND SCHEDULE

Adamsmedia

Avon, Massachusetts

Published by

Adams Media, a division of F+W Media, Inc.

57 Littlefield Street, Avon, MA 02322. U.S.A.

www.adamsmedia.com

ISBN 10: 1-4405-9523-2

ISBN 13: 978-1-4405-9523-3

eISBN 10: 1-4405-9524-0

eISBN 13: 978-1-4405-9524-0

Printed in the United States of America.

10   9   8   7   6   5   4   3   2   1

Library of Congress Cataloging-in-Publication Data

The quick and easy college cookbook.
Avon, Massachusetts: Adams Media, [2016]
LCCN 2015043727 (print) | LCCN 2016000198 (ebook) | ISBN
   9781440595233 (pb) | ISBN 1440595232 (pb) | ISBN 9781440595240 (ebook)
   | ISBN 1440595240 (ebook)
LCSH: Quick and easy cooking. | College students—Nutrition. |
   LCGFT: Cookbooks.
LCC TX833.5 .Q53256 2016 (print) | LCC TX833.5 (ebook) | DDC
   641.5/12—dc23
LC record available at http://lccn.loc.gov/2015043727

Contains material adapted from *The Everything*® *College Cookbook*, by Rhonda Lauret Parkinson, copyright © 2005 by F+W Media, Inc., ISBN 10: 1-59337-303-1, ISBN 13: 978-1-59337-303-0; *The Everything*® *Healthy Meals in Minutes Cookbook*, by Patricia M. Butkus, copyright © 2005 by F+W Media, Inc., ISBN 10: 1-59337-302-3, ISBN 13: 978-1-59337-302-3; *The Everything*® *Quick and Easy 30-Minute, 5-Ingredient Cookbook*, by Linda Larsen, copyright © 2006 by F+W Media, Inc., ISBN 10: 1-59337-692-8, ISBN 13: 978-1-59337-692-5; *The Everything*® *Easy Vegetarian Cookbook*, by Jay Weinstein, copyright © 2015 by F+W Media, Inc., ISBN 10: 1-4405-8719-1, ISBN 13: 978-1-4405-8719-1; *The Everything*® *Mediterranean Cookbook, 2nd Edition*, by Peter Minaki, copyright © 2013 by F+W Media, Inc., ISBN 10: 1-4405-6855-3, ISBN 13: 978-1-4405-6855-8; *The Everything*® *Gluten-Free College Cookbook*, by Carrie S. Forbes, copyright © 2013 by F+W Media, Inc., ISBN 10: 1-4405-6568-6, ISBN 13: 978-1-4405-6568-7; *The Everything*® *Easy Asian Cookbook*, by Kelly Jaggers, copyright © 2015 by F+W Media, Inc., ISBN 10: 1-4405-9016-8, ISBN 13: 978-1-4405-9016-0; and *The Everything*® *Busy Moms' Cookbook*, by Susan Whetzel, copyright © 2013 by F+W Media, Inc., ISBN 10: 1-4405-5925-2, ISBN 13: 978-1-4405-5925-9.

Always follow safety and commonsense cooking protocol while using kitchen utensils, operating ovens and stoves, and handling uncooked food. If children are assisting in the preparation of any recipe, they should always be supervised by an adult.

Many of the designations used by manufacturers and sellers to distinguish their products are claimed as trademarks. Where those designations appear in this book and F+W Media, Inc. was aware of a trademark claim, the designations have been printed with initial capital letters.

Cover design by Erin Alexander.

Cover images © iStockphoto.com/jatrax; Stuart Monk/margouillat/ Yulia Yunovidova/123RF.

Interior image of dish, fork and knife © iStockphoto.com/Icon_Craft_Studio.

This book is available at quantity discounts for bulk purchases.

For information, please call 1-800-289-0963.

CONTENTS

INTRODUCTION

Delicious, healthy food isn't hard to cook and it doesn't need to take a long time. With what you and your roommates have got in your kitchen (and maybe a quick trip to the corner grocery store), you can whip up something that will get you ready for back-to-back classes, an evening of studying, or a night out with friends.

The recipes you'll find here are easy and fast. There are appetizers like Potstickers for when a couple of your friends drop by, and main dishes like Meaty Spaghetti that you can whip up in between classes. There are even quick bites like English Muffin Pizzas for days when you're on the go. Under the weather or missing your parents' home-cooked meals? Comforting dishes like Potato Soup, Five-Ingredient Chili, or Mexi Mac 'n' Cheese will leave you feeling more like yourself. Recovering from a late night? Try some Chicken Noodle Soup or a Cheese Omelet to ease the pain. Pulling an all-nighter to finish that twenty-page paper? Throw together a Microwave Lasagna for an extra boost of energy.

Doing your own cooking is simple, and it'll save you money by avoiding the endless stream of takeout meals or cafeteria food. You'll find that buying groceries stretches your money further than ordering takeout. Also, by doing your own cooking you can eat what *you* want, so you're spending your money more wisely than at a restaurant.

Many of these recipes are super-healthy—like Mushroom Risotto or Tofu Ranchero—if you're vegetarian or vegan or following a gluten-free diet. And there's plenty of flavorful stuff to keep you ready for exam week: Bacon Burgers, Spicy Italian Sausage Pizza Wraps, and Meatball Pizza, among others.

To make these and other delicious dishes, you don't need a huge, fancy kitchen with tons of expensive equipment. Basic ingredients and equipment, outlined in Chapter 1, will get you started. And you don't have to be world class as far as cooking skills go. Everything in this book is quick, simple, and affordable.

So get out the pot to start some Spanish Beef Stew, get a couple of South of the Border Burgers sizzling in a pan, microwave some Microwave S'mores for dessert, or—if you just want a snack for you and your friends—put out a plate of Spicy Chicken Wings, chips and Chili-Cheese Dip, and some Crispy Fried Shrimp Balls.

It's time to do some quick and easy cooking.

WHAT YOU'LL NEED
IN YOUR KITCHEN

Leaving home for college presents challenges as well as opportunities. For students whose kitchen know-how doesn't extend beyond the reheat setting on the microwave, the idea of having to learn basic cooking skills along with calculus can seem overwhelming. It's all too easy to give in to the lure of the dining hall or food court. However, these basic tips will help turn cooking from a chore into a creative, stress-free break from studying.

Stocking the Kitchen

There are a few basic pieces of equipment that every well-equipped kitchen should have. Of course, whether or not you bring all of them to college will depend on your specific circumstances. For example, residences with communal kitchens often provide pots, pans, and other cooking essentials for residents. And there is no point in bringing a heavy-duty frying pan if you're going to be relying on a microwave oven as your primary heat source. Here is a basic list of items for setting up a kitchen, which you can add to or subtract from based on your own needs.

There are a few basic utensils you will need to stock your kitchen area. Fortunately, most are quite inexpensive and can frequently be found at discount stores. Items you absolutely need for cooking include:

- Plastic mixing bowls for mixing ingredients and serving noodle and salad dishes
- Wooden spoons for stirring and mixing
- A heatproof rubber spatula for mixing ingredients and turning food during cooking
- A plastic or metal colander for draining washed, blanched, and boiled food
- Knives, particularly a good French knife for cutting meat
- A plastic or wooden cutting board for cutting, chopping, and mincing food
- Measuring spoons and a plastic measuring cup
- A vegetable peeler and a can opener
- A grater for grating, shredding, and slicing cheese and other foods
- A pastry brush for basting food
- A wire whisk for whisking sauces and eggs

Mix It Up!

Many recipes call for food to be beaten, blended, whipped, processed, or crushed. If your budget is limited, hand tools can perform many of these functions. For example, an egg beater (also called a hand mixer) is fine for beating eggs and whipping cream. And nothing beats a mortar and pestle for grinding and crushing nuts, herbs, spices, crackers, soft fruit, and almost any food that will fit into the bowl-shaped mortar.

However, if your budget permits, you may want to explore some higher-tech options for blending and mixing. The ultimate timesaving device, a blender is perfect for harried but health-conscious students. Compact, inexpensive, and easy to clean, a blender will do everything from liquefying smoothie ingredients to puréeing vegetables. Even if your cooking requirements don't extend beyond hastily throwing together breakfast on busy weekdays, a blender will help you put together a tasty and nutritious meal in mere minutes. (You may have to drink it while walking to class, but that's okay!)

BLENDER OR FOOD PROCESSOR?

Besides the basic blender, another option for mixing food is a food processor. A food processor performs all of the functions of a blender and more. Besides grating cheese and making pastry dough, higher-end models can even be used to make bread dough. However, for most students, these extra options don't justify the food processor's higher-end price tag. Furthermore, the blender's tall shape means it can hold more liquid, which makes it a better choice for preparing smoothies and other drinks. If you have the space and can afford it, a food processor is a useful addition to your kitchen, but not essential.

Electrical Extras

Some college residences allow students to keep small electrical appliances in the dorm or the residence kitchen. A coffeemaker allows you to have a cup of java ready as soon as you wake up in the morning. Tea drinkers will want a kettle for boiling water. Along with a toaster or toaster oven, these items will help make your living quarters seem more like home.

When it comes to larger appliances, definitely consider a microwave oven or a hot plate if your budget and college regulations permit it. Basically, a hot plate performs all the functions of a stovetop-heating element, while taking up considerably less space than a conventional stove. A hot plate can be used for everything from cooking soup to frying pork chops. Although it can't completely replace a standard electric oven, a microwave oven can be used for everything from making popcorn and reheating leftovers to preparing an entire meal. Today, compact microwave and refrigerator combinations, designed specifically for dormitories, are available. Some even come with a small freezer attached.

Another handy device for dorm cooking is a rice cooker/steamer combination. Compact and inexpensive, this appliance steams meat, seafood, and vegetables, and it cooks rice and beans more quickly than the standard stovetop-heating element. As an added bonus, it has a plastic surface that makes cleaning easy. For students who have a microwave, the addition of a rice cooker/steamer can provide some of the advantages of stovetop cooking, making it unnecessary to purchase a hot plate.

Equipment for the Stovetop

A few good pots are essential for stovetop cooking. Ideally, you should have three different sizes: a smaller pot for sauces, a medium-sized pot for soups and single-serving meals, and a large pot for boiling noodles, potatoes, and cooking for a group. However, if money is an issue, it's better to purchase one pot made of quality material rather than several inexpensive pots that may not heat properly or may be hard to clean. In that case, a medium-sized pot is the most practical choice.

Make sure the saucepan is made of a heavy material that conducts heat evenly. While cast-iron and copper pots are heavier than you need (and probably beyond your budget), stainless steel wrapped in aluminum or copper is a good choice. While you can always wear oven mitts, cooking will be easier if the handles are made of a material that won't heat up during cooking, such as wood, plastic, or rubber. Finally, test the lid to make sure it fits tightly.

Not surprisingly, quality frying pans are made of the same type of material as saucepans because both are designed for stovetop cooking. A medium-sized, 12" frying pan will meet all your needs for sautéing, braising meat, and cooking eggs. As with a saucepan, it's important to make sure the frying pan comes with a tight-fitting lid.

Oven Cooking

Oven cooking requires its own special equipment that can take the high heats needed for baking, broiling, and roasting. A large, rectangular-shaped metal baking sheet is used for making cookies, while a square, deep-sided metal baking pan is used for baking bars and desserts. When it comes to muffins, there is no substitute for a standard muffin pan—consider getting more than one to prevent having to cook in batches. A glass baking dish is used for main dishes such as fish fillets and marinated chicken breasts that don't need a rack to let the fat drip off. Finally, a deep-sided casserole dish is used for one-pot meals such as rice- and noodle-based casseroles.

Kitchen Staples

Once you've purchased the basic tools needed for cooking, it's tempting to start filling up the refrigerator. Hold off until you've purchased a few dry staple ingredients. A pantry stocked with basic ingredients—such as flour—will keep you from having to make repeat emergency trips to the local grocery store every time you cook a meal. Here are the essentials:

- ○ **Flour:** As its name implies, all-purpose flour is used for almost every type of baking.
- ○ **Sugar:** Regular granulated white sugar is used both as a sweetener at the table and in cooking.
- ○ **Brown sugar:** Molasses-based brown sugar is used in baking, sauces, and wherever a recipe calls for a stronger flavor agent than granulated sugar.
- ○ **Olive oil:** Olive oil is used for sautéing and frying, and as a salad dressing and in marinades.
- ○ **Instant broth:** Chicken, beef, and vegetable broth are used in soups, casseroles, and other dishes.

- ○ **Dried herbs and spices:** Dried herbs and spices lend flavor to soups, stews, and other slow-cooked dishes.
- ○ **Salt and pepper:** Standard table salt should meet all your cooking needs, but you may want to consider purchasing a pepper mill to grind your own peppercorns.
- ○ **Noodles:** No, they don't need to be ramen! Italian pasta noodles like linguine, penne, or even standard spaghetti are a quick and easy source of protein.
- ○ **Rice:** For variety, experiment with different types such as brown and scented rice.
- ○ **Miscellaneous flavoring agents:** Lemon juice, tomato sauce, and soy sauce will allow you to create a number of different dishes.

USE OLIVE OIL

Not only is olive oil healthier than vegetable oil—scientists believe its monounsaturated fats can help ward off heart disease—it's also much more versatile. Besides being an excellent cooking oil, olive oil lends a delicate flavor to salad dressings and marinades, and can even serve as a low-fat substitute for butter on toasted bread.

Timesaving Ingredients

While nothing beats the flavor of fresh herbs or chicken broth prepared from scratch by slowly simmering a whole chicken in water, packaged and instant ingredients will save you time on busy weeknights. For example, don't let recipes that call for lemon juice put you off—most supermarkets carry lemon juice in a handy plastic lemon-shaped container. Made with oregano, basil, and other seasonings, canned tomato sauce saves you from the work of having to boil and crush tomatoes. Stored in a cool, dry place, a can of unopened tomato sauce will keep for several months.

Instant broth comes in many forms, including cubes, powdered mix, cans, and ready-to-use cartons. All are equally convenient. However, the carton types need to be refrigerated and used within two weeks after they are opened.

When it comes to noodles, many types of Asian noodles—such as rice noodles—don't even need to be boiled. Just soak them in hot or warm water until they soften. And precooked (also called "oven-ready") lasagna noodles can go straight from the package to the frying pan or casserole dish.

WHICH DRIED SPICES?

There are literally hundreds of spices. However, for those on a limited budget, a good tip is to think Italian. Nothing beats dried oregano, basil, and parsley for bringing out the flavor of simmered and slow-cooked dishes. Garlic powder and onion powder make a convenient substitute for actual onion and garlic on nights that you don't feel up to peeling, mincing, and chopping.

Shelf Life

Even dry ingredients go stale eventually. Expect flour, baking powder, and baking soda to last for up to one year. White granulated sugar has a longer shelf life than other dry ingredients—it will last up to eighteen months. On the other hand, brown sugar lasts for only six months. Of course, improper storage will cause ingredients to go stale more quickly. Worse, certain types of small bugs—such as the flour beetle—feed on dry ingredients. For best results, store your staples in tightly sealed canisters.

Don't worry about blowing your budget on a matching set of fancy chrome or other metal canisters. Plastic is fine, as long as it has a tight seal. Don't have room in your dorm for a full set of canisters? Set one canister aside to serve as a storage space for smaller amounts of various ingredients. Store each ingredient in a plastic bag, seal it, and place the bag in the canister.

Meal Planning 101

Preparing a detailed grocery list makes it much easier to stick to a budget. But where do you begin? The best way is to start by preparing a meal plan for one or two weeks. Try to pick more than one recipe that uses the same ingredients so that you can save money by purchasing in bulk. Let's say, for example, that you decide to cook Five-Ingredient Chili and Mexican Fried

---

Rice. Including both recipes in the same grocery shopping trip lets you purchase larger portions of everything from ground beef to tomato sauce.

Of course, you'll want to incorporate leftovers into your meal plan. But refrigerated leftovers have to be eaten within days, and eating the same meal twice in one week can get a little boring. Fortunately, there are ways around this problem.

For recipes designed to provide two or more servings, one option is to cook two half-portions of the recipe, slightly altering the ingredients for each half. For example, with Five-Ingredient Chili you could prepare a half-portion, cutting the ingredients in half but otherwise following the recipe exactly. Then prepare a second half-portion, but substitute chickpeas for the kidney beans and replace the beef with ground turkey or chicken. This gives you more variety, making it easier to resist the temptation to skip dinner in favor of the snack machine conveniently located just down the hall.

When halving or doubling a recipe, it's helpful to know how to convert cups into tablespoons, tablespoons into teaspoons, and vice versa. The following table contains several conversions.

EQUIVALENT MEASURES

Measurement	Equivalent Measure
3 teaspoons	1 tablespoon
4 tablespoons	¼ cup
5 tablespoons plus 1 teaspoon	⅓ cup
8 tablespoons	½ cup
10 tablespoons plus 2 teaspoons	⅓ cup
12 tablespoons	¾ cup
16 tablespoons	1 cup
48 teaspoons	1 cup
1 cup	8 ounces
1 quart	32 ounces

Shopping Tips

When writing up a grocery list, many people find it helps to organize ingredients in the same way that items are organized in the grocery store. Fresh vegetables are categorized together, as are canned vegetables, frozen foods, and meat products. Items located at either end of the store are either first or last on the list. Organizing the grocery list in this way ensures that you're moving in an organized fashion from one end of the store to the other, instead of wandering back and forth between aisles.

Here are a few tips for cutting costs at the grocery store:

○ Never shop when you're tired or hungry. This makes it easier to avoid expensive "impulse buying."
○ Always bring a list and stick to it.
○ Check the "sell by" and "use by" dates on perishable items such as milk and meat. Always purchase food with the most recent date so that it will last longer.
○ Be sure to ask for a rain check if the store is out of an advertised special.
○ Always store perishable goods in the refrigerator or freezer as soon as possible so there is no danger of spoilage.
○ Many larger supermarkets have frequent-shopper programs that give substantial discounts to regular customers. Check to see if you are eligible for a frequent-shopper card.

Finally, if your refrigerator comes with a freezer compartment, be sure to use it. This will give you more variety—even if you live far from the ocean, shrimp and other types of shellfish are readily available frozen. A freezer also allows you to buy fresh meat and seafood in bulk and freeze individual portions.

The Freshman Weight Gain

Statistics show that approximately half of all students put on between ten and fifteen pounds during their first year of college and university. It's easy to fall victim to the "Freshman 15" when you're living on your own for the first time, trying to adjust to a busy schedule, and fast-food vendors are scattered across campus. However, putting on weight will just increase the stress that you're already feeling from academic pressures, and it can be hard to take off later.

The benefits of a vigorous exercise session go beyond the calories expended during the workout. Exercising increases the body's metabolic rate, causing you to burn up calories at a faster rate even after you've finished your workout. The effect can last for up to two full days.

Here are a few tips for keeping the pounds away: First and foremost, stick to a regular meal schedule. If you are planning a lengthy study session away from the dorm, prepare healthy snacks to take with you. Simple snacks such as granola bars, cheese and crackers, and trail mix all provide energy without the fat and calories in potato chips and chocolate.

Plan your meals at least one week in advance. One option is to cook ahead, making all your weekly meals on the weekend. It's much easier to stick to a healthy meal plan on a busy weeknight when all you need to do is heat up dinner instead of cooking it. Finally, take time to exercise. Many colleges and universities have excellent exercise facilities right on campus that are free for students. With a little planning, you can fit an exercise session into your daily schedule. A daily swim or aerobics workout makes it easier to control your weight, and it also lifts your spirits by releasing endorphins, giving you a much-needed boost of energy.

BREAD AND BREAKFAST

Basic Scrambled Eggs and Bacon

▶ SERVES 2

4 slices bacon
2 teaspoons butter
3 large eggs
Dash heavy cream
Salt, to taste
Freshly ground black pepper, to taste

1. Cut bacon strips in half. Heat a small nonstick skillet over medium-high heat. Add bacon strips in a single layer and cook until starting to brown on the underside, about 3 minutes. Flip slices and cook until crispy, about 2 minutes. Transfer bacon to a plate lined with paper towels to drain.

2. Melt butter in a medium-sized nonstick skillet over medium heat. Whisk eggs and cream in a bowl and season to taste with salt and pepper. Pour egg mixture into the skillet and cook to desired doneness, stirring occasionally.

3. Equally divide eggs and bacon onto 2 warm plates and serve immediately.

Scrambled Eggs with Cheese

▶ SERVES 6

12 large eggs, beaten
¼ cup light cream
¼ cup mascarpone cheese
½ teaspoon salt
⅛ teaspoon white pepper
¼ teaspoon dried marjoram leaves
3 tablespoons butter
1 cup shredded Havarti or Swiss cheese

1. In a large bowl, combine eggs with cream, mascarpone cheese, salt, pepper, and marjoram. Beat with eggbeater or hand mixer until smooth.

2. Heat butter in large skillet over medium heat. Add egg mixture. Cook eggs, stirring occasionally, until they are set, about 10–12 minutes. Add Havarti cheese, cover pan, and remove from heat. Let stand for 2–3 minutes, then remove lid, stir cheese gently into eggs, and serve.

Scrambled Eggs with Chorizo

▶ SERVES 4

8 ounces uncooked Mexican chorizo sausage
10 large eggs
$\frac{1}{4}$ cup whole milk
$\frac{1}{4}$ teaspoon seasoned salt
Freshly ground black pepper, to taste
1 cup salsa

1. Remove casings from sausage. Heat a large nonstick skillet over medium-high heat and cook sausage until starting to brown, about 5–6 minutes, stirring frequently. Break up larger pieces of meat while cooking.

2. Break eggs into a medium-sized mixing bowl. Add milk and whisk until blended. Season with salt and pepper. Move chorizo to one side of the pan and add eggs to the open area. Stir into chorizo. Cook until eggs are scrambled and set, about 4 minutes. Serve hot with salsa on the side.

Scrambled Egg Burritos

▶ SERVES 4

1 tablespoon unsalted butter
1 cup finely chopped onion
$\frac{1}{2}$ cup sliced roasted peppers
9 extra-large eggs, beaten
$\frac{1}{2}$ cup half-and-half
1–2 dashes of hot pepper sauce
2 cups shredded jalapeño jack cheese
Salt and ground black pepper, to taste
4 (12") flour tortillas
1 cup salsa

1. In a large skillet over medium heat, melt butter; add onions and sliced roasted peppers. Cook until onions are soft and translucent, about 5 minutes.

2. In a medium bowl, combine eggs and half-and-half, and add them to the pan. Cook, stirring constantly with a wooden spoon, until eggs are about half cooked—still very runny; add hot pepper sauce, cheese, salt, and pepper. Remove from heat. Eggs should be soft, creamy, and have small curds.

3. Soften tortillas by placing them directly atop the stove burner on medium heat; a few black spots are okay. Spoon ¼ of egg mixture slightly off center on a tortilla. Fold the sides in upon egg and roll tortilla away from yourself, folding filling in and tucking with your fingers to keep even pressure. Repeat with remaining tortillas. Serve with salsa.

Huevos Rancheros

▶ SERVES 4

1 can Mexican-style black beans in sauce
2 cups salsa
8 large eggs
$\frac{1}{2}$ cup half-and-half
$\frac{1}{2}$ teaspoon salt
Unsalted butter, for greasing pan
8 (8" diameter) soft corn tortillas
1 cup shredded Monterey jack or mild Cheddar cheese
$\frac{1}{2}$ cup sour cream
Chopped cilantro

1. Heat the beans and salsa in separate saucepans over low heat.
2. In a medium bowl, beat together eggs, half-and-half, and salt. Melt butter in a nonstick pan; add egg mixture and cook over low heat until soft and creamy, with small curds.
3. Soften tortillas either by steaming or warming in the microwave. Place 2 tortillas onto each plate. Divide hot black beans evenly onto these tortillas. Spoon eggs onto beans, then sauce with a ladleful of salsa. Garnish with cheese, sour cream, and cilantro. Serve immediately.

Herb-Baked Eggs

▶ SERVES 4

3 ounces ham, thinly sliced
3 large eggs
1 teaspoon Dijon mustard
¼ cup plain yogurt
¾ cup shredded Cheddar cheese
2 teaspoons chopped fresh chives
2 teaspoons chopped fresh parsley
Herb sprigs, for garnish

1. Preheat oven to 375°F.
2. Lightly grease 4 (6-ounce) ramekins with butter. Line ramekins with ham slices.
3. Combine eggs, Dijon, and yogurt, and mix well. Stir ¼ cup of cheese into egg mixture. Add half the chives and parsley to egg mixture, and stir well. Spoon mixture into prepared ramekins. Sprinkle with remaining cheese and herbs.
4. Bake for 20–25 minutes, until golden and set. Garnish with herb sprigs and serve hot.

Jalapeño-Cheddar Frittata

▶ SERVES 10

12 extra-large eggs
$\frac{1}{4}$ cup half-and-half
$\frac{1}{2}$ teaspoon seasoned salt
Freshly ground black pepper, to taste
$\frac{1}{2}$ cup sliced pickled jalapeños
2 tablespoons butter
$2\frac{1}{2}$ cups shredded Cheddar cheese

1. Preheat oven to 350°F.

2. Combine eggs, half-and-half, salt, and pepper in a medium-sized mixing bowl. Use an electric mixer to beat until very light.

3. Pat jalapeño slices dry with a paper towel. Melt butter in a medium-sized ovenproof nonstick skillet over medium heat. Scatter jalapeños evenly on the bottom of the skillet. Sprinkle evenly with cheese.

4. Pour eggs over cheese in the skillet. Place skillet on a rimmed baking sheet and bake for 20–25 minutes, until just firm. Let cool for several minutes, until set, before removing from the pan. Cut into wedges and serve hot.

Basil Vegetable Frittata

▶ SERVES 6

8 large eggs
3/4 cup whole milk
1/2 cup seeded and chopped tomato
6 ounces button mushrooms, sliced
2 tablespoons chopped fresh basil
1/2 teaspoon salt
1/2 teaspoon ground black pepper
1/2 cup grated Parmesan cheese
Chopped fresh parsley, for garnish

1. Preheat oven to 375°F.
2. Combine eggs and milk in a large bowl and whisk until well blended. Add tomatoes, mushrooms, basil, salt, and pepper, and stir to combine.
3. Lightly butter a 9" square nonstick baking pan. Pour egg mixture into prepared pan and top with Parmesan cheese. Bake 20–22 minutes, or until lightly browned and eggs are set. Allow to rest for 1–2 minutes, sprinkle with parsley, and serve hot.

Smoked Salmon and Cream Cheese Frittata

▶ SERVES 4

8 large eggs
$\frac{1}{2}$ cup whole milk
$\frac{1}{4}$ cup chopped fresh chives
$\frac{1}{4}$ cup chopped fresh basil
$\frac{1}{2}$ teaspoon black pepper
$\frac{1}{8}$ teaspoon salt
2 teaspoons vegetable oil
2 ounces cold cream cheese, cut into $\frac{1}{2}$" pieces
3 ounces thinly sliced smoked salmon, chopped

1. Combine eggs, milk, chives, basil, pepper, and salt in a medium-sized bowl and mix until smooth.

2. Position broiler rack about 6" from the heat source. Preheat broiler to medium.

3. Heat oil in a medium-sized, ovenproof nonstick skillet over moderate heat until hot but not smoking. Pour egg mixture into the skillet and sprinkle cream cheese pieces on top. Cook, using a spatula to lift up cooked egg around the edges to let raw egg flow underneath. Cook for 3–5 minutes, until frittata is set on bottom and egg is almost set but still moist on top.

4. Remove from heat and sprinkle the salmon over frittata, lightly pressing the salmon into the surface.

5. Place skillet in oven and broil frittata until set, slightly puffed, and golden in patches, about 1–1$\frac{1}{2}$ minutes.

6. Let cool for 5 minutes. Loosen edge with a spatula and slide frittata onto a large plate. Cut into wedges and serve at room temperature.

Peach Pancakes

2 ripe peaches, peeled and diced
4 tablespoons sugar, divided
$\frac{1}{4}$ teaspoon cinnamon
$\frac{3}{4}$ cup flour
1 teaspoon baking powder
1 large egg, separated
$\frac{3}{4}$ cup milk
1 teaspoon vanilla
2 tablespoons butter

1. In small bowl, toss peaches with 2 tablespoons sugar and cinnamon. In a medium bowl, combine flour, remaining 2 tablespoons sugar, baking powder, egg yolk, milk, and vanilla and stir just until combined.

2. Beat egg white until stiff; fold into flour mixture, then fold in peach mixture. Heat a skillet over medium heat and grease it with the butter.

3. Use a $\frac{1}{4}$-cup measure to scoop out batter, and pour onto hot, greased skillet. Cook pancakes until edges start to look dry and cooked and bubbles form on surface, about 2–4 minutes. Carefully flip pancakes and cook until second side is light brown, 1–2 minutes longer.

Sausage Rolls

▶ YIELDS 24 ROLLS

24 pork sausage links
1 (17-ounce) package frozen puff pastry, thawed
1 cup grated Cheddar cheese
½ cup grated Parmesan cheese
1 teaspoon dried thyme leaves
1 egg, beaten
¼ teaspoon salt

PUFF PASTRY

Puff pastry is found frozen near the pie shells and cakes in your supermarket. Follow the directions for thawing and using the pastry. Many brands require thawing overnight in the refrigerator so the butter that is encased in the layers of pastry doesn't melt. Keep a couple of boxes on hand to make easy snacks.

1. Preheat oven to 400°F. Line cookie sheets with parchment paper and set aside. In a heavy skillet, cook pork sausage links over medium heat until golden brown and cooked, about 5–7 minutes. Remove to paper towels to drain.

2. Unfold puff pastry sheet and place on a lightly floured surface. In a small bowl, combine cheeses and thyme leaves and toss to combine. Sprinkle this mixture over the puff pastry and gently press cheese mixture into surface; roll to a 12" × 18" rectangle. Cut into 3 (12" × 6") rectangles, then cut each rectangle in half to make 6 squares. Cut each square into 4 (3" × 3") squares. Place a cooked and drained sausage on the edge of each square and roll up to enclose sausage; press pastry to seal.

3. In small bowl, beat egg with salt and brush over sausage rolls. Place on prepared cookie sheets and bake for 12–18 minutes until puffed and golden brown. Serve hot.

Breakfast Baklava French Toast

▶ SERVES 2

3 large eggs

2 tablespoons orange juice

1 teaspoon grated orange zest

$\frac{1}{8}$ teaspoon vanilla extract

$\frac{1}{4}$ cup plus 1 tablespoon honey, divided

2 tablespoons whole milk

1 teaspoon ground cinnamon, divided

$\frac{1}{4}$ cup chopped walnuts

$\frac{1}{4}$ cup chopped blanched almonds

$\frac{1}{4}$ teaspoon ground cloves

1 tablespoon sugar

2 tablespoons white bread crumbs or ground Melba toast

4 slices bread

2 tablespoons unsalted butter

1 teaspoon confectioners' sugar

1. In a large bowl, whisk together eggs, orange juice, zest, vanilla, $\frac{1}{4}$ cup honey, milk, and $\frac{1}{4}$ teaspoon cinnamon. Reserve.

2. Pulse walnuts and almonds in a food processor until they are finely crumbled. Transfer nuts to a small bowl and add cloves, $\frac{1}{2}$ teaspoon cinnamon, sugar, and bread crumbs. Stir to combine.

3. Sandwich half the walnut-and-almond mixture between 2 slices of bread. Repeat with the remaining 2 slices. Carefully dunk both sides of the sandwiches into egg mixture. Make sure egg mixture soaks into the bread.

4. Add butter to a large skillet over medium heat and heat 30 seconds. Add sandwiches and fry 2 minutes per side or until golden.

5. Place each sandwich on a plate and cut them diagonally. Dust with confectioners' sugar. Top with remaining honey and sprinkle with $\frac{1}{4}$ teaspoon cinnamon. Serve immediately.

Stuffed French Toast

▶ SERVES 4

4 tablespoons melted butter, divided
$\frac{1}{2}$ cup mascarpone cheese, divided
$\frac{1}{4}$ cup strawberry preserves
8 slices cracked wheat bread
2 large eggs
1 teaspoon vanilla
$\frac{1}{4}$ teaspoon cinnamon

1. Preheat broiler. Spread 3 tablespoons melted butter in a rimmed baking sheet and set aside. In a small bowl, combine $\frac{1}{4}$ cup mascarpone cheese and preserves and mix.

2. Spread preserves mixture on 4 bread slices and top with remaining slices. Cut these sandwiches in half to make triangles.

3. In a shallow bowl, beat remaining $\frac{1}{4}$ cup mascarpone cheese until fluffy, then add eggs, remaining 1 tablespoon melted butter, vanilla, and cinnamon, and beat until smooth. Dip sandwiches in egg mixture, turning to coat.

4. Place coated sandwich triangles in butter on baking sheet. Broil 6" from heat source for 4–5 minutes, then carefully turn the sandwiches and broil for 3–5 minutes longer on second side until golden brown and crunchy. Serve immediately.

Fruit-Stuffed French Toast

▶ SERVES 6

½ teaspoon olive oil

3 medium loaves challah bread, sliced into 6 (3") slices

½ cup sliced strawberries

½ cup blueberries

1 cup diced peaches

2 large eggs

4 large egg whites

¼ cup skim milk

1 cup orange juice

¼ cup nonfat plain yogurt

¼ cup confectioners' sugar

1. Preheat oven to 375°F. Grease a baking sheet with oil.

2. Cut a slit into the bottom crust of each bread slice to form a pocket.

3. Mix strawberries, blueberries, and peaches in a medium bowl. Fill each pocket with about ⅓ cup fruit mixture. Press the pocket closed.

4. In a large shallow bowl, beat eggs, egg whites, and milk. Dip bread into egg mixture, letting it fully absorb the mixture. Place bread on prepared baking sheet. Bake 20 minutes, flipping bread halfway through.

5. While bread is baking, boil orange juice in a small saucepan over medium heat until reduced by half and mixture is syrupy, about 15 minutes.

6. Remove French toast from oven, transfer to plates, and cut each slice in half diagonally. Serve each with a dollop of yogurt, a drizzle of juice, and a sprinkling of sugar.

Camper's Breakfast

▶ SERVES 8

1 cup diced cured sausage
¼ cup water
3 large potatoes, peeled and diced
1 large onion, peeled and sliced
1 large green bell pepper, seeded and sliced
1 large red bell pepper, seeded and sliced
1 teaspoon smoked paprika
¾ teaspoon salt, divided
½ teaspoon ground black pepper
½ teaspoon fresh thyme leaves
1 cup grated Graviera or Gruyère cheese
4 tablespoons extra-virgin olive oil, divided
8 large eggs

1. In a large skillet over medium-high heat, add sausage and water. Cook 3 minutes or until water evaporates and sausage is crispy. Add potatoes and stir to coat in the sausage drippings. Reduce heat to medium and cook another 5 minutes.

2. Add onions, bell peppers, and smoked paprika. Cook 3 more minutes. Season with ½ teaspoon salt, black pepper, and thyme. Reduce heat to medium-low and cook 10–15 minutes or until potatoes are fork-tender. Sprinkle with cheese and take the pan off the heat. The residual heat will melt the cheese.

3. In another skillet, add 2 tablespoons oil and fry each egg to your liking (sunny-side up or over easy). Season eggs with remaining salt.

4. To serve, place a scoop of sausage-onion mixture onto each plate and a fried egg on top. Drizzle with remaining oil. Serve hot.

Roasted Potatoes with Vegetables

▶ SERVES 6

2 tablespoons olive oil
3 medium baking potatoes, peeled and chopped
1 medium sweet potato, peeled and chopped
3 large carrots, peeled and chopped
1 medium yellow onion, peeled and chopped
$\frac{1}{2}$ pound button mushrooms
1 teaspoon salt
1 teaspoon ground black pepper

1. Preheat oven to 400°F.
2. In a large bowl, combine oil, potatoes, carrots, onions, and mushrooms. Stir to mix. Transfer vegetables to a large roasting pan and sprinkle with salt and pepper.
3. Roast until tender, 30–45 minutes. Serve warm or at room temperature.

Fresh Fruit and Yogurt

▶ SERVES 6

6 cups plain nonfat yogurt
$\frac{1}{4}$ medium cantaloupe, seeded and chopped
$\frac{1}{4}$ medium honeydew melon, seeded and chopped
2 medium kiwis, peeled and sliced
1 medium peach, pitted and sliced into wedges
1 large plum, pitted and sliced into wedges
$\frac{1}{2}$ pint fresh raspberries
6 mint sprigs

Spoon yogurt into serving bowls and arrange fruit decoratively around each rim. Garnish with mint.

Spinach Quiche

▶ SERVES 6

1 unbaked 9" pie shell
$\frac{1}{4}$ cup green onions, chopped
2 tablespoons unsalted butter
1 (1-pound) package fresh spinach, washed, stems removed, roughly
    chopped
Pinch of nutmeg
$\frac{1}{2}$ teaspoon salt
$\frac{1}{4}$ teaspoon freshly ground black pepper
3 large eggs
6 ounces half-and-half or milk
$\frac{1}{4}$ cup shredded Gruyère or Swiss cheese

1. Heat oven to 350°F.
2. Gently place wax paper over the unbaked pie shell and fill the
   cavity with dried beans or pie beads. Bake until golden brown,
   15–20 minutes (this is known as "blind baking" the crust). Cool
   on a rack; remove beans and paper.
3. Increase oven temperature to 375°F.
4. Heat green onions and butter in a skillet until they sizzle. Add
   spinach, nutmeg, salt, and pepper; cook until spinach is wilted.
5. Whisk together eggs and half-and-half in a medium bowl. Add the
   spinach mixture.
6. Sprinkle half of the cheese into the prebaked pie crust; add the
   spinach-egg mixture. Top with remaining cheese; bake for 35 minutes,
   until the top is domed and beginning to brown.

Pumpkin Bread

▶ SERVES 10

2 cups boiled and mashed pumpkin
1 cup white sugar
1 cup brown sugar
$1/2$ cup oil
1 large egg
$2^1/2$ cups flour
$1/2$ teaspoon salt
$1/2$ teaspoon cinnamon
$1/2$ teaspoon cloves
$1/4$ teaspoon nutmeg
2 teaspoons baking soda
1 cup chopped pecans

1. Preheat oven to 350°F. Grease a 9" × 5" loaf pan.
2. In a large bowl, combine pumpkin, sugars, oil, and egg. Mix well.
3. In a medium bowl, combine the remaining ingredients, except nuts, and mix well. Add to pumpkin mixture. Stir in nuts.
4. Bake in prepared loaf pan for 1 hour. Test periodically by inserting a toothpick into the center of the loaf; when the toothpick comes out clean, the bread is done.

Banana Nut Bread

SERVES 10

1¼ cups all-purpose flour

1 teaspoon baking soda

¼ teaspoon baking powder

½ teaspoon cinnamon

½ teaspoon salt

1 cup sugar

2 large eggs

½ cup oil

3 overripe medium bananas, mashed (1¼ cups)

1 teaspoon vanilla extract

¾ cup coarsely chopped walnuts, toasted lightly in a dry pan until fragrant

1. Heat oven to 350°F. Butter a 9" × 5" loaf pan.

2. In a mixing bowl, whisk together flour, baking soda, baking powder, cinnamon, and salt.

3. In a separate bowl, whisk together sugar, eggs, and oil; whip vigorously until creamy and light in color, about 5 minutes. Add mashed bananas and vanilla extract to the egg mixture.

4. Add flour mixture to wet ingredients in three additions, mixing only as much as necessary to incorporate the ingredients, since overmixing will toughen the batter. Stir in nuts, and pour batter into prepared pan.

5. Bake in center of oven until the top is springy and a toothpick inserted in the center comes out clean, about 50–60 minutes. Allow to cool for 10 minutes; transfer to a rack to cool completely before slicing.

APPETIZERS, SIDES, AND SAUCES

Spicy Meatballs

▶ SERVES 8–10

1 (16-ounce) package frozen mini meatballs
1 tablespoon olive oil
1 onion, peeled and chopped
¼ teaspoon salt
Dash white pepper
¾ cup chili sauce
½ cup peach jam
¼ cup water

1. Bake meatballs as directed on package. Meanwhile, heat olive oil in a heavy saucepan and add onion, salt, and pepper. Cook and stir until onion is starting to turn brown and caramelize.

2. Stir in chili sauce, peach jam, and water, and bring to a boil. Add the cooked meatballs and stir to coat. Serve.

Garlic Stuffed Cherry Tomatoes

▶ YIELDS 30

30 cherry tomatoes
3 ounces cream cheese, softened
¼ cup whipped salad dressing or mayonnaise
2 tablespoons roasted garlic paste
⅓ cup grated Parmesan cheese

1. Cut off tops of cherry tomatoes and, using a small teaspoon, scoop out flesh, leaving shell intact. Drain upside down on paper towels.

2. In small bowl, beat cream cheese until soft and fluffy. Add salad dressing, roasted garlic paste, and Parmesan cheese; beat well. Stuff a teaspoon of this mixture into each cherry tomato. Serve immediately or cover and refrigerate up to 4 hours.

Hummus

▶ YIELDS 2 CUPS

4 cloves garlic
2 tablespoons extra-virgin olive oil
1 (15-ounce) can chickpeas, drained
$\frac{1}{4}$ cup tahini
2 tablespoons lemon juice
$\frac{1}{4}$ cup sour cream
$\frac{1}{2}$ teaspoon salt
$\frac{1}{8}$ teaspoon red pepper flakes

1. Peel garlic cloves but leave whole. Place in a small heavy saucepan along with olive oil over medium heat. Cook the garlic until it turns light brown, stirring frequently, for about 5–8 minutes; watch carefully. Remove from heat and let cool for 10 minutes.

2. Combine the garlic and oil with all remaining ingredients in blender or food processor and blend or process until smooth. Spread in a serving dish, drizzle with a bit more olive oil, and serve immediately with pita chips.

Spicy Mixed Nuts

▶ YIELDS 2 CUPS

$\frac{1}{4}$ cup butter

2 tablespoons brown sugar

1 teaspoon salt

$\frac{1}{4}$ teaspoon cayenne pepper

$\frac{1}{8}$ teaspoon white pepper

2 tablespoons Worcestershire sauce

2 cups mixed nuts

1. In heavy saucepan, melt butter with brown sugar, salt, spices, and Worcestershire sauce. Cook mixture over low heat until blended, stirring frequently. Place nuts in single layer on microwave-safe baking sheet and drizzle the butter mixture over them. Toss gently but thoroughly.

2. Microwave the mixture on high power for 5–9 minutes, stirring 3 times during cooking, until nuts are darkened and crisp and butter is absorbed. Cool on paper towels, then store in airtight container.

Baked Feta

▶ SERVES 4

1 (4" × 4" × 1") slab feta cheese

2 tablespoons extra-virgin olive oil, divided

1 large Roma tomato, thinly sliced

1 large banana or bell pepper, seeded and thinly sliced

$\frac{1}{4}$ teaspoon red pepper flakes

$\frac{1}{4}$ teaspoon dried oregano

1. Preheat oven to 400°F. Place feta and 1 tablespoon oil in a small baking dish. Top with alternating layers of tomato and pepper slices. Drizzle remaining oil and sprinkle red pepper flakes and oregano over vegetables.

2. Cover baking dish tightly with tinfoil and bake 20 minutes. Serve immediately.

Fried Peppers

▶ SERVES 4

1 pound long, slender red or green
    peppers (sweet or hot)
$\frac{1}{4}$ cup extra-virgin olive oil, divided
1 teaspoon salt
1 tablespoon red or white wine vinegar

1. Poke peppers with a fork a few times
   all over. Heat 2 tablespoons oil in a
   large skillet over medium-high heat.
   Fry peppers (in batches) 3–4 minutes
   per side until skins are lightly golden.

2. Transfer peppers to a tray lined with
   paper towels and season with salt.
   Serve on a plate with a drizzle of
   vinegar and the remaining oil. Serve
   warm or at room temperature.

Spicy Chicken Wings

▶ SERVES 4

4 cloves garlic, peeled and minced

1 small onion, peeled and grated

1 tablespoon grated lemon zest

1 tablespoon lemon juice

$\frac{1}{4}$ teaspoon ground cinnamon

$\frac{1}{4}$ teaspoon smoked paprika

$\frac{1}{2}$ teaspoon ground allspice

1 teaspoon ground black pepper

2 teaspoons salt

2 tablespoons fresh thyme leaves

$\frac{1}{4}$ cup extra-virgin olive oil

2 pounds chicken wings, patted dry

GRILLED CHICKEN WINGS

Chicken wings are also great cooked on a grill, if you have access to one. Preheat a gas or charcoal grill to medium-high. Place wings on grill and cook 4–5 minutes per side or until juices run clear. Serve immediately.

1. In a large bowl, combine all ingredients except chicken wings. Add chicken wings and stir to coat.

2. Marinate wings at least 4 hours or overnight in the refrigerator. Remove wings from refrigerator 20 minutes before grilling so they come up to room temperature. Remove excess marinade from the wings.

3. Preheat oven to 425°F and set the rack at the third position from the top. Line a baking sheet with greased tinfoil or parchment paper. Bake wings for 20 minutes and then flip them. Bake them for another 15 minutes or until crispy and brown.

Marinated Portobello Mushrooms

▶ SERVES 6

6 portobello mushrooms
1 teaspoon extra-virgin olive oil
2 teaspoons balsamic vinegar
$\frac{1}{8}$ teaspoon salt
$\frac{1}{4}$ teaspoon ground black pepper
$\frac{1}{4}$ cup roughly chopped fresh marjoram
$\frac{1}{4}$ cup roughly chopped fresh oregano

1. Remove stems from the caps of mushrooms and scrape out black membrane. Slice stems in half and reserve for later use in a stock.

2. Mix together remaining ingredients in a large bowl or zip-top bag. Add mushroom caps, cover or seal bag, and marinate at least 3 hours at room temperature.

3. Preheat oven to 400°F.

4. Transfer mushrooms to a baking sheet lined with tinfoil. Roast mushrooms 15–20 minutes. Cut caps into small wedges before serving.

Potstickers

½ pound ground pork
1 cup finely shredded cabbage
2 green onions, sliced
2 teaspoons minced ginger
2 tablespoons soy sauce
1 teaspoon sesame oil
½ teaspoon ground black pepper
24 dumpling wrappers
2 tablespoons vegetable oil
¼ cup water
¼ cup chopped green onions, for garnish

STOCK YOUR FREEZER

Potstickers can be made ahead and frozen. Prepare the dumplings through step 2, then lay out the potstickers on a baking sheet and place in the freezer. Once frozen, transfer the potstickers to a container or resealable bag. They can be stored in the freezer for up to 1 month. When ready to prepare, continue with step 3, but add a few additional minutes to the cooking time.

1. In a large bowl, combine pork, cabbage, green onions, ginger, soy sauce, sesame oil, and pepper. Refrigerate for 30 minutes.

2. Take 1 dumpling wrapper and use your finger to brush water along edge of circle. Place about 1 tablespoon of mixture in center of wrapper. Fold dumpling wrapper over and firmly press the sides to seal completely. Repeat for remaining wrappers. While you are forming the potstickers, create a flattened bottom. You can also pleat the edges with a fork.

3. Heat oil in a wok over medium heat. Place potstickers, flattened-side down, in one layer and fry for 1–2 minutes.

4. Carefully pour water into the wok and cover. Allow pot stickers to steam for an additional 2–3 minutes. Remove the lid and continue cooking until the water has evaporated.

5. Place potstickers on a plate and sprinkle the tops with green onions. Serve hot.

Spring Rolls

▶ SERVES 12

½ pound pork tenderloin, shredded
2 tablespoons oyster sauce, divided
½ teaspoon baking soda
6 dried mushrooms
1 tablespoon chicken broth or stock
½ teaspoon sugar
4 cups plus 3½ tablespoons vegetable oil, divided
1 cup mung bean sprouts, rinsed and drained
1 cup grated carrot
2 medium green onions, trimmed and thinly sliced on the diagonal
¼ teaspoon sesame oil
12 spring roll wrappers
2 tablespoons cornstarch mixed with 1 tablespoon water

1. In a medium bowl, marinate pork in 1 tablespoon oyster sauce and baking soda for 30 minutes.

2. Soak dried mushrooms in hot water for 20 minutes to soften; drain and thinly slice.

3. In a separate bowl, combine remaining 1 tablespoon oyster sauce, chicken broth, and sugar. Set aside.

4. Add 2 tablespoons of oil to a preheated wok or skillet. When oil is hot, add marinated pork. Stir-fry briefly until it changes color and is nearly cooked through, 2–3 minutes. Remove from wok.

5. Add 1½ tablespoons of oil to wok. When oil is hot, add drained mushrooms. Stir-fry for 1 minute, then add bean sprouts, carrot, and green onions. Add prepared sauce in middle of wok and bring to a boil. Add pork and mix through. Drizzle with sesame oil. Cool.

Spring Rolls—continued

6. In wok, heat 4 cups of oil to 375°F. While oil is heating, prepare spring rolls: To wrap, lay wrapper in a diamond shape. Place a tablespoon of filling in the middle. Coat all edges with cornstarch-and-water mixture. Roll up wrapper and tuck in edges. Seal tucked-in edges with cornstarch and water. Continue with the remainder of the spring rolls. (Prepare more cornstarch and water as necessary.)

7. Deep-fry spring rolls 2 at a time until they turn golden. Drain on paper towels.

Chili-Cheese Dip

▶ SERVES 12

1 (15-ounce) can vegetarian chili
¼ cup diced onions
½ cup diced tomatoes
1 (8-ounce) package cream cheese or vegan cream cheese
1 cup Cheddar cheese or vegan Cheddar
1 teaspoon garlic powder

VEGETARIAN CHILI

Most major grocery stores sell canned vegetarian chili. One of the easiest to find is Hormel Vegetarian Chili with Beans, which contains textured vegetable protein instead of meat.

1. In a 4-quart slow cooker, place all ingredients.

2. Stir gently; cover, and heat on low for 1 hour.

Crispy Fried Shrimp Balls

▶ SERVES 6

$\frac{1}{2}$ pound shrimp, peeled and deveined

1 tablespoon fish sauce

1 large egg white

1 teaspoon ground black pepper

1 tablespoon cornstarch

1 tablespoon plus 2 cups vegetable oil, divided

1 package wonton wrappers, sliced into thin strips

$\frac{1}{2}$ cup Thai sweet chili sauce

1. In a food processor, pulse shrimp, fish sauce, egg white, black pepper, cornstarch, and 1 tablespoon oil several times until mixture turns into a paste, but still has some small pieces of shrimp.

2. Place wonton strips in a layer on a cutting board.

3. Form shrimp paste into balls approximately $1\frac{1}{4}$ tablespoons in size. You may need to wet your hands in between to keep the balls from sticking.

4. Roll each ball into the wonton strips so that they cover the entire ball. Repeat until all balls have been wrapped.

5. Heat remaining 2 cups oil in a wok to 375°F. In batches, fry shrimp balls until they turn golden brown, approximately 3–4 minutes. Drain fried balls on plates lined with paper towels. Serve hot with Thai sweet chili sauce.

Bacon, Lettuce, and Tomato Cups

▶ SERVES 6

2 cucumbers, seedless variety
4 strips bacon
$\frac{1}{2}$ cup finely chopped romaine lettuce
$\frac{1}{8}$ cup finely diced tomato, flesh only, no seeds
$\frac{1}{8}$ cup shredded Cheddar cheese
$\frac{1}{4}$ cup mayonnaise
$\frac{1}{4}$ teaspoon seasoned salt
Freshly ground black pepper, to taste
Chopped fresh parsley, for garnish

1. To prepare cucumbers, rinse under cool running water and pat dry. Trim off and discard about 1" from each end of both cucumbers (the ends are often bitter). You can either peel cucumbers entirely or "stripe" them by leaving alternating strips of green peel.

2. Prepare 12 cucumber cups by cutting cucumbers into slices about 1"–1¼" thick; use a melon baller to scoop out the center of each slice, about ¾" deep. Place cups upside down in a single layer on paper towels for about 10 minutes before using.

3. Place several layers of paper towels on a microwave-safe plate or tray and place bacon strips in a single layer on top. Cover bacon with a paper towel to prevent spattering. Microwave on medium-high at 1-minute intervals for a total of 3–4 minutes or until bacon is crispy. Rotate bacon ¼ turn at each cooking interval. (If cooking bacon on stovetop, cook until crispy and transfer to paper towels to drain.)

4. Chop cooked bacon into medium dice and transfer to medium-sized mixing bowl. Add lettuce, tomatoes, Cheddar, mayonnaise, salt, and pepper; lightly blend with a fork until evenly mixed. The mixture should be tossed until just combined, not mashed down with the fork.

5. To assemble, arrange cups on a serving platter. Use a teaspoon to fill each cup with bacon mixture until nicely mounded on the top. Garnish with chopped parsley and serve.

Spicy Fiesta Chicken in Cucumber Cups

▶ SERVES 6

2 cucumbers, seedless variety

$2/3$ cup diced rotisserie chicken

$1/3$ cup shredded pepper jack or equivalent Mexican cheese

$1/2$ cup hot habanero salsa or spicy salsa

$1/2$ cup finely chopped romaine lettuce

2 tablespoons chopped fresh cilantro, plus extra for garnish

$1/3$ cup finely diced red onion

$1/4$ teaspoon garlic salt

1. To prepare cucumbers, rinse under cool running water and pat dry. Trim off and discard about 1" from each end of cucumbers (the ends are often bitter). You can either peel cucumbers entirely or "stripe" them by leaving alternating strips of green peel.

2. Prepare 12 cucumber cups by cutting cucumbers into slices about 1"–1¼" thick; use a melon baller to scoop out the center, about ¾" deep. Place cups upside down in a single layer on paper towels for about 10 minutes before using.

3. Combine chicken, cheese, salsa, lettuce, cilantro, onion, and garlic salt in medium-sized mixing bowl; toss with a fork until just combined.

4. To assemble, arrange cups on a serving platter. Use a teaspoon to fill each cup with chicken mixture until nicely mounded on the top. Garnish with chopped cilantro leaves and serve.

Madras Deviled Eggs

▶ SERVES 2

2 extra-large eggs

2 tablespoons mayonnaise

1½ tablespoons sour cream

1½ teaspoons Madras curry powder

⅛ teaspoon (or to taste) cayenne pepper

¼ teaspoon ground cumin

1 tablespoon minced Major Grey's Chutney (or other mango chutney)

1 tablespoon chopped fresh chives

1 tablespoon freshly squeezed lime juice

Paprika, for garnish

1. Place eggs in medium-sized saucepan and add enough cold water to cover eggs by at least 1". Bring to medium boil over medium-high heat and cook for 12 minutes. Run cold water over eggs to cool, then peel and cut in half lengthwise.

2. While eggs are cooking, mix filling ingredients. Combine mayonnaise, sour cream, curry powder, cayenne, cumin, chutney, chives, and lime juice in a small bowl and use a fork to blend into a paste. Add the cooked egg yolks and blend. Use either a small scoop or a pastry bag fitted with a star tip to pipe the filling into the egg whites. Sprinkle with paprika. Serve immediately, or place in an airtight container and refrigerate.

Garlic Feta Spread

 SERVES 6

$\frac{1}{2}$ pound feta cheese, crumbled
3 cloves garlic, peeled and pressed
2 tablespoons extra-virgin olive oil
2 tablespoons finely chopped fresh parsley
1 teaspoon dried oregano
$\frac{1}{2}$ teaspoon ground black pepper

Combine all ingredients in a medium bowl. Mash with a fork and mix well until combined. Refrigerate or serve at room temperature.

Feta and Pepper Spread

 SERVES 8

2 tablespoons extra-virgin olive oil
1 medium onion, peeled and sliced
1 large green bell pepper, seeded and chopped
1 large red bell pepper, seeded and chopped
$\frac{1}{2}$ pound feta cheese (1 thick slice)
1 teaspoon dried oregano
$\frac{1}{2}$ teaspoon ground black pepper

1. Preheat oven to 350°F.
2. Heat oil in a large skillet over medium-high heat. Sauté onion and bell peppers until soft, about 8 minutes.
3. Place feta in a small baking dish and top with onion-pepper mixture. Sprinkle oregano and black pepper over top. Cover dish and bake 15 minutes. Serve hot.

Greek Islands Feta and Herb Spread

 SERVES 6

2 tablespoons olive oil

2 teaspoons freshly squeezed lime juice

$\frac{1}{2}$ teaspoon chopped fresh rosemary

1 teaspoon dried Italian seasoning

$\frac{1}{4}$ teaspoon garlic salt

Freshly ground black pepper, to taste

6 ounces crumbled feta cheese

8 ounces plain yogurt

Chopped fresh parsley, for garnish

1. Combine olive oil, lime juice, rosemary, Italian seasoning, garlic salt, and pepper in serving bowl. Set aside at room temperature for 20 minutes to allow flavors of dried herbs to blossom.

2. Add feta and yogurt to the seasoning mixture and combine thoroughly. Refrigerate until ready to use. Sprinkle with chopped parsley just before serving.

Parsley Spread

SERVES 8

4 slices stale bread, crusts removed

2 cups chopped fresh parsley leaves

3 green onions, ends trimmed, chopped

½ cup extra-virgin olive oil

¼ cup fresh lemon juice

1 tablespoon vinegar

1 teaspoon dried oregano

1 teaspoon salt

½ teaspoon ground black pepper

1. In a medium bowl, moisten bread with a little water. Squeeze to drain excess water.

2. Pulse parsley and green onions in a food processor to combine. Slowly add bread, oil, lemon juice, vinegar, oregano, salt, and pepper. Continue pulsing until smooth. Refrigerate or serve at room temperature.

Mushroom Bruschetta

▶ SERVES 4

1 baguette or crusty country bread

4 teaspoons aioli or mayonnaise mixed with chopped garlic

12 ounces mixed mushrooms, such as button, oyster, shiitake, enoki, or portobello

2 tablespoons olive oil (or butter; not vegan)

1 teaspoon mixed dried herbs, such as thyme, oregano, rosemary, and basil

Juice of $\frac{1}{2}$ medium lemon

Kosher salt and freshly ground black pepper, to taste

Fresh chopped parsley or chives (optional)

1. Heat a stovetop grill (or an oven to 400°F). Slice bread on a diagonal into 8 (1"-thick) oblong slices; spread aioli onto both sides of each slice. Grill or bake bread slices until dark brown marks decorate their faces, top and bottom. Transfer to a serving plate.

2. Cut mushrooms into large, uneven chunks and slices, and mix all varieties together. Warm a large, heavy skillet over high heat. Add mushrooms to the dry pan all at once, then add olive oil (or butter); sprinkle herbs on top. Cook without stirring for the first 4–5 minutes, allowing mushrooms to get a brown crust. After 5 minutes, stir to mix in herbs, and cook until accumulating liquid is mostly evaporated. Season well with lemon, salt, and pepper.

3. Spoon onto grilled bread, and garnish with chopped parsley or chives if desired.

Curry Dip

▶ MAKES 2½ CUPS

1 teaspoon olive oil

½ cup finely chopped onion

½ medium jalapeño pepper, seeded and finely chopped (about 1 teaspoon)

2 teaspoons finely chopped red bell pepper

1 teaspoon Madras curry powder

1 teaspoon ground cumin

½ teaspoon ground coriander

½ teaspoon ground turmeric

Pinch of cayenne pepper

¼ teaspoon salt, plus more to taste

1 tablespoon very fresh, soft raisins

1½ cups soy mayonnaise (or regular mayonnaise; not vegan)

1 tablespoon chopped fresh cilantro

A few drops fresh lemon juice

Ground black pepper, to taste

WHAT IS "CURRY POWDER"?

What you know as "curry powder" is actually a blend of spices, invented by the British to resemble one of the famous masalas (spice blends) of India. In addition to ground coriander, cumin, mustard seed, turmeric, and other spices, good Madras curry (such as Sun Brand) contains ground, dried curry (or "kari") leaves, which are a typical spice of southern and southwestern India. Most authentic Indian recipes call not for curry powder, but a combination of spices (a masala) specifically designed for that dish.

1. Put the oil in a small skillet over medium heat. Add onions, jalapeño, and bell pepper; cook stirring occasionally until onion is translucent, about 5 minutes.

2. Add curry powder, cumin, coriander, turmeric, cayenne, and ¼ teaspoon salt. Cook 1 minute more, until spices are very fragrant. Add raisins and about 1 tablespoon of water. Remove from heat.

3. Transfer to a food processor. Chop on high speed for 30 seconds; scrape down sides of bowl with a rubber spatula. Add soy mayonnaise and cilantro; process 30 seconds more, until smooth and even. Adjust seasonings with lemon juice, salt, and black pepper.

Josh's Mushroom Dip

 SERVES 8

1 teaspoon olive oil
1 large portobello mushroom cap
1 (10-ounce) package white mushrooms
1/2 packet dried onion soup mix
1 pint sour cream
8 cups assorted raw vegetables, such as carrots, celery, mixed bell
    peppers, zucchini, and yellow squash, cut into sticks

1. Heat olive oil in a small skillet over medium-high heat; cook portobello until tender, about 5 minutes. Cool it, and chop it finely.

2. Chop white mushrooms finely, either by hand or by pulsing in a food processor in batches of 5 at a time.

3. In a medium bowl, stir onion soup mix into sour cream. Fold in chopped mushrooms.

4. Transfer to a bowl, and serve surrounded by raw vegetables for dipping.

Olive and Red-Pepper Dip

SERVES 8

1/2 cup pitted green olives
1 roasted red pepper, chopped
1 teaspoon balsamic vinegar
2/3 cup soft bread crumbs

2 cloves garlic, peeled and smashed
1/2 teaspoon red pepper flakes
1/3 cup extra-virgin olive oil

1. In a food processor, combine all ingredients except oil. Pulse to combine but leave the mixture chunky.

2. With the processor running, slowly add oil until it is well combined. Refrigerate or serve at room temperature.

Warm Pepper Jack and Bacon Dip

▶ SERVES 4

5 ounces bacon
2 cups shredded pepper jack cheese
1 cup cream cheese or light cream cheese, at room temperature
$\frac{1}{4}$ cup Madeira
$\frac{1}{3}$ cup sliced green onions (about $\frac{1}{4}$" slices)

1. Heat a medium-sized nonstick skillet over medium-high heat and add bacon. Cook until crispy, stirring frequently, about 8 minutes. Use a slotted spoon to transfer the bacon to paper towels to drain. When cool, crumble into small pieces.

2. Combine the pepper jack cheese, cream cheese, and Madeira in a microwave-safe serving dish. Microwave on high for 90 seconds or until bubbly (cooking time will vary according to microwave power). Stir in the bacon pieces, top with green onions, and serve with crispy vegetables, such as blanched asparagus spears or celery sticks, or beef or chicken skewers.

Grilled Asparagus

1 pound asparagus
2 tablespoons butter
1 tablespoon garlic-flavored olive oil

1 teaspoon seasoned salt
$\frac{1}{8}$ teaspoon pepper

1. Hold asparagus spears between your hands and bend until they snap; discard the tough ends.

2. Preheat oven to 425°F. In small saucepan, melt butter with oil, salt, and pepper. Brush asparagus with this mixture, then place in a single layer on a baking sheet. Roast asparagus, brushing frequently with butter mixture, for approximately 10 minutes, or until tender. Serve immediately.

Chilled Broccoli Trio

2 cups broccoli florets, parboiled
2 cups chopped broccoli rabe, parboiled
2 cups chopped Chinese broccoli, parboiled
4 cloves garlic, peeled and chopped
1 cup toasted walnuts
$\frac{1}{2}$ cup crumbled Gorgonzola cheese
$\frac{1}{2}$ cup balsamic salad dressing
Salt and ground black pepper, to taste
Red pepper flakes, to taste

1. Combine the three broccolis in a large mixing bowl and toss with garlic. Chill until ready to serve.

2. Just before serving, add walnuts, cheese, dressing, salt, pepper, and red pepper flakes. Toss well.

Baby Potato Toss

SERVES 6

1 pound baby red-skinned potatoes
$1/2$ cup butter
3 cloves garlic, peeled and minced
2 tablespoons fresh thyme leaves
2 tablespoons chopped fresh parsley
$1/4$ teaspoon salt
$1/8$ teaspoon white pepper

1. Peel a strip of skin from the middle of each potato. Place potatoes in large pot and cover with cold water. Cover and bring to a boil over high heat. Uncover, lower heat, and cook potatoes until tender when pierced with a fork, about 12–14 minutes.

2. Meanwhile, combine butter and garlic in a small saucepan. Cook over medium heat for 2–3 minutes, until garlic is fragrant. Remove from heat.

3. When potatoes are done, drain thoroughly; then return potatoes to the hot pot. Let stand off the heat for 2–3 minutes, shaking occasionally. Place pot over medium heat and pour butter mixture over potatoes. Sprinkle with remaining ingredients, toss gently, and then serve.

Appetizers, Sides, and Sauces

Stir-Fried Broccoli with Garlic

▶ SERVES 3

2 tablespoons olive oil
2 cloves garlic, peeled and finely chopped
$\frac{1}{2}$ teaspoon red pepper flakes, or to taste
$\frac{1}{2}$ pound broccoli florets
$\frac{1}{8}$ teaspoon salt, or to taste
2 tablespoons water
1 red bell pepper, seeded, cut into chunks
2 teaspoons lemon juice
2 tablespoons soy sauce

1. Heat the olive oil in a large skillet on medium-high heat. Add garlic cloves and red pepper flakes.
2. Add broccoli. Stir briefly, sprinkling salt over broccoli while cooking, until florets turn bright green.
3. Add water and let broccoli cook 2–3 more minutes.
4. Add red bell pepper. Stir in lemon juice and soy sauce. Cook, stirring, for another minute. Serve immediately.

Szechuan Stir-Fried Cabbage with Hot Peppers

▶ SERVES 4–6

¼ cup plus 2 tablespoons peanut or other neutral oil
8 dried red chili peppers, quartered and seeded
1 (1") piece fresh ginger, peeled and finely chopped
1 medium head Chinese cabbage, chopped into 2" pieces
½ teaspoon cornstarch
1 tablespoon soy sauce
1 teaspoon dry sherry or Chinese cooking wine
1 teaspoon sugar
1 teaspoon rice wine vinegar
1 teaspoon Asian sesame oil

1. Heat ¼ cup of oil in a wok or skillet over high heat. Stir in peppers and fry, stirring, for 1 minute, until peppers darken in color. Transfer peppers and oil to a bowl and set aside.

2. Pour remaining 2 tablespoons of oil into the wok; add ginger and cook for a few seconds until fragrant. Add cabbage all at once. Fry, stirring, for 1 minute.

3. Combine cornstarch, soy sauce, and sherry together in a small bowl. Add to wok. Stir until cornstarch cooks and forms a thick sauce; add sugar and vinegar. Sprinkle in sesame oil and pour in peppers and their oil. Stir to combine well. Transfer to a serving bowl.

Braised Carrots

1 pound carrots	$\frac{1}{2}$ teaspoon salt
$\frac{3}{4}$ cup water	$\frac{1}{8}$ teaspoon white pepper
$\frac{1}{4}$ cup orange juice	$\frac{1}{4}$ teaspoon dried marjoram leaves
1 tablespoon sugar	2 tablespoons butter

1. Peel carrots and cut diagonally into 1½" chunks; set aside. In a heavy saucepan, combine remaining ingredients. Bring to a boil over medium heat.

2. Add carrots to the pan and cover. Reduce heat to low and simmer carrots, covered, for 5–8 minutes, until carrots are soft when pierced with a knife. Remove the carrots from the pan and place on serving plate. Increase heat to high and bring liquid to a boil. Boil for 3–5 minutes, until liquid is reduced and syrupy. Pour over carrots and serve.

Honey Orange Carrots

SERVES 4–6

1 (16-ounce) package baby carrots

2 cups water

2 tablespoons orange juice concentrate

2 tablespoons honey

2 tablespoons butter

$\frac{1}{4}$ teaspoon dried thyme leaves

1. Rinse carrots and place in medium saucepan with water. Bring to a boil over high heat, then lower heat to medium and simmer carrots for 5–8 minutes, until just tender.

2. Drain carrots and return to pan. Stir in orange juice concentrate, honey, and butter; cook and stir over medium heat until sauce thickens and coats carrots, 2–4 minutes. Add thyme leaves and simmer for a minute, then serve.

Garlicky Green Beans

SERVES 6

1 pound green beans
4 cups water
1 tablespoon olive oil
1 tablespoon butter
6 cloves garlic, peeled and chopped
1 shallot, peeled and chopped
$\frac{1}{2}$ teaspoon salt

TYPES OF GARLIC

There are several forms of garlic that you can buy. Garlic powder is powdered dried garlic; $\frac{1}{8}$ teaspoon is equal to one clove. Garlic salt is garlic powder combined with salt; $\frac{1}{4}$ teaspoon is equal to one clove. And garlic paste in a tube is puréed, concentrated garlic; 1 teaspoon is equal to one clove of garlic.

1. Trim the ends off green beans and cut each bean in half crosswise. Place in heavy saucepan and cover with water. Bring to a boil over high heat, then lower heat to medium and simmer for 5–8 minutes, until beans are crisp-tender.

2. Meanwhile, combine olive oil and butter in heavy saucepan, and add garlic and shallot. Cook and stir over medium heat until the garlic is fragrant and turns light brown around the edges.

3. Drain beans and add to garlic mixture in pan along with salt. Cook and stir over medium heat for 2–3 minutes, until beans are coated. Serve immediately.

Green Beans with Red Peppers

▶ SERVES 6

2 tablespoons olive oil

1 onion, peeled and finely chopped

3 cups frozen green beans

1 red bell pepper, cut into strips

1 tablespoon lemon juice

$\frac{1}{2}$ teaspoon salt

$\frac{1}{2}$ teaspoon dried thyme leaves

1. In heavy saucepan, heat olive oil over medium heat. Add onion; cook until onion is tender, stirring frequently.

2. Meanwhile, prepare green beans as directed on package and drain well. Add red bell pepper to saucepan with onions; cook and stir for 2–4 minutes, until tender. Add beans, lemon juice, salt, and thyme leaves; stir gently and cook until hot, about 2–3 minutes longer. Serve immediately.

Lemon Garlic Green Beans

▶ SERVES 4

Nonstick olive oil cooking spray

$1\frac{1}{2}$ pounds green beans, trimmed

3 tablespoons olive oil

3 large shallots, peeled and cut into thin wedges

6 cloves garlic, peeled and sliced

1 tablespoon grated lemon zest

$\frac{1}{2}$ teaspoon salt

$\frac{1}{2}$ teaspoon ground black pepper

$\frac{1}{2}$ cup water

Spray a 4- to 5-quart slow cooker with cooking spray. Place green beans in slow cooker. Add remaining ingredients over beans. Cook on high 4–6 hours or on low 8–10 hours.

Roasted Sugar Snap Peas

▶ SERVES 6

3 cups sugar snap peas
2 tablespoons olive oil
$\frac{1}{2}$ teaspoon dried marjoram
$\frac{1}{2}$ teaspoon garlic salt
$\frac{1}{8}$ teaspoon pepper

1. Preheat oven to 425°F. Remove strings from sugar snap peas, if desired. Place on baking sheet and sprinkle with remaining ingredients. Mix with your hands until peas are coated.
2. Roast for 4–6 minutes, until peas just begin to brown in spots and are crisp and tender. Serve immediately.

Duchess Potatoes

▶ SERVES 8

1 (12-ounce) package refrigerated mashed potatoes
1 large egg, beaten
$\frac{1}{4}$ cup plus 2 tablespoons grated Parmesan cheese, divided
2 tablespoons sour cream
$\frac{1}{2}$ teaspoon dried basil leaves
2 tablespoons milk

1. Preheat oven to 375°F. In large bowl, combine all ingredients except milk and 2 tablespoons Parmesan cheese and beat well until combined. Spoon or pipe mixture into 16 mounds onto parchment paper–lined cookie sheets. Brush with milk and sprinkle with 2 tablespoons Parmesan cheese.
2. Bake potatoes for 15–20 minutes or until tops are beginning to brown and potatoes are hot. Serve immediately.

Appetizers, Sides, and Sauces

Garlic Mashed Potatoes

 SERVES 6

4 medium red potatoes
4 tablespoons butter or margarine
$\frac{1}{4}$ cup milk
2 teaspoons garlic powder, or to taste
$\frac{1}{2}$ teaspoon of salt, or to taste

1. Wash and peel potatoes. Cut roughly into bite-sized chunks.

2. Place potatoes in a deep microwave-safe dish and cover with water.

3. Microwave potatoes on high heat for 10 minutes. Give the dish a quarter turn and continue microwaving for 1–2 minutes at a time until potatoes are cooked through and can easily be pierced with a fork. (Total cooking time should be about 15 minutes.) Drain.

4. Place potatoes in a large bowl. Add butter or margarine and use a fork or a potato masher to whip potatoes. Gradually add milk until potatoes have reached the desired consistency (do not add more milk than is needed). Stir in garlic powder and salt to taste and serve.

Smashed Potatoes

▶ SERVES 6-8

6 russet potatoes
¼ cup butter
4 cloves garlic, peeled and minced
⅓ cup whole milk
½ teaspoon salt
1 tablespoon chopped fresh basil leaves

**THE FLUFFIEST
MASHED POTATOES**

Adding butter to the
potatoes before adding
liquid helps ensure that
the potatoes will be fluffy.
The fat in the butter helps
coat the starch granules in
the potatoes so they don't
absorb too much liquid and
become sticky or gluey.
Use this rule every time you
make mashed or smashed
potatoes for best results.

1. Peel potatoes and cut into 1" cubes;
as you work, place the potatoes in a
large saucepan filled with cold water.
When all the potatoes are prepared,
bring to a boil over high heat. Cover
pan, lower heat, and simmer potatoes
for 15–20 minutes, until potatoes are
tender when pierced with fork.

2. Meanwhile, combine butter and garlic in small saucepan and cook over
medium heat, stirring frequently, until garlic is fragrant and tender,
about 2 minutes. Remove from heat. In another small saucepan,
combine milk, salt, and basil and heat until steam forms.

3. When potatoes are tender, drain thoroughly, then return potatoes
to hot pan and shake for 1 minute over medium heat. Add butter
mixture and mash with a potato masher. Then add milk mixture and
stir gently. Serve immediately.

Roasted Yukon Gold Potatoes

▶ SERVES 4

1 medium onion, peeled and roughly chopped
2 tablespoons olive oil
¼ cup chopped parsley
3–4 cloves garlic, peeled and minced
1½ pounds Yukon Gold potatoes, washed, sliced ½" thick
1 teaspoon salt
Ground black pepper, to taste

1. Heat oven to 425°F.
2. Put onion, olive oil, parsley, and garlic in blender or food processor, and purée until smooth. Toss with potatoes and salt, then wrap in a ready-made foil oven bag or a sheet of tinfoil crimped to seal. Potatoes should be no more than 2 layers deep.
3. Bake on a sheet pan, in center rack for 45 minutes, until potatoes are tender when poked with a fork. Season with pepper and serve.

Leek Potato Cakes

▶ SERVES 4

2 cups finely chopped leeks, white part only
2 cups finely grated peeled potatoes
$\frac{1}{2}$ teaspoon dried sage
2 large eggs, beaten
2 tablespoons flour
1 teaspoon salt
$\frac{1}{4}$ teaspoon freshly ground black pepper
Olive oil for frying

1. Wash leeks very thoroughly to remove any grit. Combine potatoes, leeks, sage, eggs, flour, salt, and pepper in a mixing bowl; mix well. Form into 8 (3") pancakes.

2. Heat $\frac{1}{4}$" of olive oil in a heavy skillet over medium heat until a piece of leek sizzles when added. Transfer 4 pancakes into the pan and cook gently, without moving them, until a crisp brown crust develops, about 5 minutes. Turn and brown other side; drain on paper towels, and repeat with remaining cakes.

Crisp Potato Pancakes

SERVES 4

1 large egg
3 large baking potatoes, peeled
1 medium onion, peeled
1 teaspoon salt
1 tablespoon flour
Clarified butter (ghee) or olive oil
    for frying

1. Beat egg in a large bowl. Using large-hole side of a box grater, shred potatoes in long motions, forming the lengthiest shreds possible. Quickly grate in onion. Add salt and sprinkle in flour; toss with your hands to combine well.

2. Heat clarified butter or oil until it shimmers but does not smoke (a piece of potato should sizzle upon entry). Form 8 pancakes from batter and pan-fry them in batches of 3–4, squeezing out excess water before gently sliding them into the pan. Cook slowly, without moving them for the first 5 minutes; then loosen with a spatula. Turn after about 8 minutes, when top appears ⅓ cooked. Finish cooking on other side, about 4 minutes more. Drain on paper towels.

WHY BUTTER IS BETTER FOR CRISPING POTATO CAKES

For browning and crispness, clarified butter achieves the best results. This may be because residual proteins in the butter caramelize on foods, or it may simply be the high temperatures that clarified butter can reach without burning. When sautéing, you can start off with a neutral oil, such as peanut oil, and add a nugget of whole butter to get a better brown.

French Fries

2 pounds (about 5) high-starch potatoes, such as Idaho baking potatoes
   or Yukon Golds, peeled
Peanut oil for frying
Salt, to taste

1. Cut potatoes into 2½"-long strips, ½" wide and thick; soak in enough
   cold water to cover them for 30 minutes. Drain and dry with absorbent
   towels.

2. Heat oil to 350°F. Fry potatoes in small batches until they are soft and
   tender enough to mash between your fingers, about 2 minutes (make
   sure to allow time between each batch for the oil to come back up to
   temperature—a fry thermometer is essential); drain on paper towels.
   The potatoes may be fried again once cooled (about 5 minutes), or set
   aside to be refried later.

3. Heat the oil to 365°F. Fry again in small batches, stirring lightly
   with a tool so they don't stick together. When golden brown (about
   2–3 minutes), remove from oil, shake off any excess, and drain on
   paper towels. Sprinkle immediately with salt, and serve in a napkin-
   lined basket.

Praline Sweet Potatoes

▶ SERVES 6

2 (16-ounce) cans sweet potatoes in syrup
$\frac{1}{2}$ cup brown sugar, divided
$\frac{1}{2}$ cup butter, divided
$\frac{1}{4}$ cup reserved sweet potato liquid
$\frac{1}{2}$ cup chopped cashews
3 tablespoons flour
$\frac{1}{8}$ teaspoon nutmeg

1. Drain sweet potatoes, reserving $\frac{1}{4}$ cup liquid. Place drained sweet potatoes in saucepan over medium heat along with $\frac{1}{4}$ cup brown sugar, $\frac{1}{4}$ cup butter, and $\frac{1}{4}$ cup reserved liquid. Mash potatoes as they heat, stirring frequently. Place in a microwave-safe casserole dish.

2. In small bowl, combine cashews, remaining $\frac{1}{4}$ cup brown sugar, flour, and nutmeg and mix well. Melt remaining $\frac{1}{4}$ cup butter and add to cashew mixture; mix until crumbly and set aside.

3. Microwave potatoes on high power for 2 minutes, then stir well. Sprinkle with cashew mixture and microwave on high 5–7 minutes longer, or until potatoes are hot. Serve immediately.

Crunchy Puréed Squash

▶ SERVES 6

1 (12-ounce) package frozen puréed winter squash
$\frac{1}{4}$ cup orange juice
2 tablespoons maple syrup
$\frac{1}{2}$ teaspoon salt
Dash white pepper
1 cup granola

1. In large saucepan, combine frozen squash with orange juice and bring to a simmer. Cook for 6–8 minutes, until the squash begins to thaw. Stir in maple syrup, salt, and pepper; continue cooking for 3–4 minutes longer, until squash is hot and smooth.
2. Place in 2-quart casserole dish and sprinkle with granola. Bake at 400°F for 12–15 minutes, until hot and granola browns slightly.

Stir-Fried Zucchini

▶ SERVES 2

1 tablespoon vegetable oil
1 large zucchini, cut on the diagonal into 1" slices
$\frac{1}{4}$ teaspoon salt
$\frac{1}{4}$ teaspoon ground black pepper
1 tablespoon soy sauce

1. Heat a wok or skillet over medium-high heat until it is nearly smoking. Add oil.
2. When oil is hot, add zucchini. Sprinkle salt and pepper over zucchini. Stir-fry for 1 minute, then stir in soy sauce.
3. Stir-fry zucchini until it turns dark green and is tender but still crisp (about 3 minutes). Serve hot.

Roasted Zucchini

 SERVES 4

1 tablespoon olive oil

2 cups zucchini rounds (about $\frac{1}{2}$" thick)

$\frac{1}{2}$ teaspoon salt

Freshly ground black pepper, to taste

2 tablespoons minced red onion

1 garlic clove, peeled and minced

1 teaspoon lemon zest

1. Preheat oven to 425°F.

2. Combine olive oil, zucchini, salt, and pepper in an 8" × 8" baking dish with sides. Use a rubber spatula to stir and coat zucchini evenly with oil and seasonings. Bake, uncovered, for about 12 minutes, stirring once midway through cooking.

3. Add red onion, garlic, and lemon zest, stirring to combine. Bake until the zucchini is tender, about 5 minutes. Transfer to a serving platter and serve hot.

Zucchini Marinara

SERVES 4

2 tablespoons olive oil
$\frac{1}{2}$ cup chopped yellow onion
2 cups sliced zucchini (about $\frac{1}{2}$"-thick rounds)
Salt, to taste
Freshly ground black pepper, to taste
1 cup marinara sauce
$\frac{1}{4}$ cup shredded mozzarella cheese
Chopped fresh parsley, for garnish

1. Heat oil in a medium-large nonstick skillet over medium-high heat. Add onions and cook until soft, about 4 minutes.

2. Add zucchini and salt and pepper to taste; cook, stirring frequently, for 4 minutes.

3. Add marinara sauce and bring to a simmer; cook until zucchini is tender when pierced with a fork.

4. Top with shredded mozzarella, cover, and heat until cheese melts, about 3 minutes. Top with parsley and serve immediately.

Korean-Inspired Marinade

 MAKES ½ CUP

2 tablespoons orange juice

2 tablespoons soy sauce

1 tablespoon honey

1 tablespoon brown sugar

1 tablespoon rice wine or sherry

1 tablespoon sesame oil

¼ teaspoon ground black pepper

½ medium Asian pear, finely grated

1 green onion, sliced

1 teaspoon toasted sesame seeds

1. Prepare your meat (or other protein) for stir-frying, cutting according to the recipe directions.

2. In a large bowl, whisk together the marinade ingredients. Place the meat in the bowl, ensuring that it has been evenly coated. Cover the bowl and allow the meat to marinate in the refrigerator for at least 1 hour. Use in your favorite stir-fry recipe, or in the Korean-inspired recipes in Chapter 7.

Orange Sauce

▶ MAKES ⅔ CUP

6 tablespoons orange juice
1 tablespoon fresh orange zest
2 tablespoons water
1 tablespoon rice vinegar
1 tablespoon dark soy sauce
2 teaspoons light soy sauce
2 teaspoons brown sugar
¼ teaspoon red pepper flakes

Combine all ingredients in a bowl. Either use immediately in a stir-fry recipe or store in a sealed container in the refrigerator until ready to use. (Use the sauce within 3–4 days.)

Simple Stir-Fry Sauce

▶ MAKES ½ CUP

3 tablespoons soy sauce
3 tablespoons water
1 tablespoon oyster sauce
2 teaspoons red wine vinegar
2 teaspoons sugar
1 teaspoon garlic salt
¼ teaspoon ground black pepper

Combine all ingredients in a small bowl. Use as called for in a recipe, or store in a sealed container in the refrigerator until ready to use. (Use the sauce within 3–4 days.)

SALADS

Apple and Greens Salad

$\frac{1}{3}$ cup light olive oil
3 tablespoons apple cider vinegar
$\frac{1}{4}$ cup sugar
$\frac{1}{2}$ teaspoon celery seed
$\frac{1}{4}$ teaspoon salt
$\frac{1}{8}$ teaspoon pepper
2 apples, cored and sliced
4 cups butter lettuce, torn into bite-sized pieces
1 cup curly endive

In small bowl, combine oil, vinegar, sugar, celery seed, salt, and pepper and mix well with wire whisk to blend. Place apples, lettuce, and endive in serving bowl and pour dressing over salad; toss gently to coat. Serve immediately.

Bacon and Spinach Salad

SERVES 6–8

4 strips bacon
1 pound baby spinach leaves
1 cup cubed Havarti cheese
$\frac{1}{2}$ cup mayonnaise

$\frac{1}{2}$ cup buttermilk
$\frac{1}{2}$ teaspoon seasoned salt
$\frac{1}{8}$ teaspoon white pepper

1. In medium saucepan, cook bacon until crisp. Drain on paper towels until cool enough to handle, then crumble. Combine cooked bacon, spinach, and cheese in serving bowl.

2. In small bowl, combine mayonnaise, buttermilk, salt, and pepper and mix well with wire whisk to blend. Drizzle half of dressing over spinach mixture and toss to coat. Serve with remaining dressing.

Basic Egg Salad

MAKES ⅔ CUP

1 tablespoon cream cheese, softened

¼ cup mayonnaise

1 tablespoon finely minced onion

4 large hard-boiled eggs, peeled and
  chopped

1 tablespoon sweet pickle relish, slightly
  drained

Salt and ground black pepper, to taste

1. In a medium bowl combine softened cream cheese with mayonnaise and onion and mix well.

2. Add chopped egg and relish. Add salt and pepper to taste. Chill before serving.

THE SECRET TO MAKING PERFECT HARD-BOILED EGGS

The perfect hard-boiled egg has a delicate white and a fully cooked yolk, without even a hint of the unattractive gray shadow that affects improperly cooked eggs. The perfect hard-boiled egg is also easy to peel. To achieve this, put the eggs in enough cold water to cover them by 1" and boil for 1 minute only. Then remove from heat, cover the pan, and let it sit undisturbed for exactly 15 minutes. Transfer the eggs to a bath of ice water for another 15–20 minutes. They should then peel easily.

Caesar Salad

▶ SERVES 8

1 large egg yolk
1 tablespoon Dijon mustard
2 tablespoons lemon juice
2 cloves garlic, peeled and finely chopped
½ cup peanut oil
¼ cup grated Parmigiano-Reggiano cheese
Pinch cayenne pepper (optional)
Salt and ground black pepper to taste
1 medium head romaine lettuce, torn into bite-sized pieces
1 cup croutons
1 small wedge Parmigiano-Reggiano cheese (optional)

1. In a mixing bowl or food processor, combine egg yolk, mustard, lemon juice, and garlic. Vigorously whisk or process in the oil, starting just a drop at a time, gradually drizzling it in a small stream, until all is emulsified into a smooth mayonnaise. Stir in cheese, cayenne, salt and pepper, and a little extra lemon juice if desired.

2. Place lettuce and croutons in a large bowl, and toss with dressing. Divide onto 8 plates, arranging croutons on top. If desired, shave curls of Parmigiano over each salad, using a vegetable peeler. Dressing may be made up to 1 week in advance and refrigerated.

Fruit and Cheese Salad

 SERVES 6

2 nectarines
2 cups sliced strawberries
2 cups blueberries
1 cup cubed Havarti cheese
$\frac{1}{2}$ cup poppy seed salad dressing

Slice nectarines and discard pits. Combine with remaining ingredients in a serving bowl and toss gently to coat. Serve immediately or cover and refrigerate up to 2 hours before serving.

Classic Ham Salad

 SERVES 3

1 pound deli ham slices
2–3 tablespoons mayonnaise
2 tablespoons dill pickle relish
1 tablespoon Dijon mustard
Salt, to taste
Freshly ground black pepper, to taste

Grind the deli ham in a food processor fitted with a metal blade, or chop very finely. Combine all ingredients in a medium-sized mixing bowl, using only 1–2 tablespoons of mayonnaise, and blend with a fork. If needed, add more mayonnaise, 1 teaspoon at a time, to achieve desired consistency. Taste and adjust seasoning as desired. Refrigerate until ready to serve.

Classic Greek Salad

▶ SERVES 4

4 romaine lettuce leaves, washed, drained, and torn

$1/2$ red onion, peeled, cut into thin rings

12 cherry tomatoes, cut in half

1 English cucumber, thinly sliced

1 green bell pepper, seeded, cut into chunks

3 tablespoons extra-virgin olive oil

2 tablespoons red wine vinegar

1 teaspoon sugar

$1/4$ teaspoon ground black pepper

$1/2$ teaspoon sea salt

$1/2$ teaspoon bottled minced garlic

$1/4$ teaspoon dried oregano, or to taste

1 cup crumbled feta cheese

12 whole olives, pitted and chopped

GREEK SALAD

A staple on Greek restaurant menus around the world, traditional Greek salad (horiatiki) is made with tomatoes, cucumbers, Greek oregano, and an olive oil dressing. Although they are popular additions, feta cheese and plump Kalamata olives are optional.

1. In a large salad bowl, combine lettuce, red onion, tomatoes, cucumber, and bell pepper.
2. In a small bowl, whisk together olive oil, red wine vinegar, sugar, pepper, sea salt, garlic, and oregano.
3. Drizzle olive oil dressing over the salad.
4. Sprinkle crumbled feta on top.
5. Add olives. Serve immediately.

Asian Beef Salad

 SERVES 4

$\frac{1}{2}$ cup mayonnaise

2 tablespoons teriyaki sauce

$\frac{3}{4}$ pound cooked beef tenderloin, trimmed, sliced, and cut into strips

$\frac{1}{2}$ cup sliced button mushrooms

$\frac{1}{4}$ cup water chestnuts, rinsed and drained

$\frac{1}{4}$ cup Chinese peapods, rinsed and stemmed

$\frac{1}{4}$ cup red bell pepper, stemmed, seeded, and cut into matchsticks

$\frac{1}{4}$ cup thinly sliced green onions

Pinch garlic salt

Freshly ground black pepper, to taste

Fresh cilantro leaves, for garnish

Mix together mayonnaise and teriyaki sauce. Place all remaining ingredients in a medium-sized bowl. Add about $\frac{3}{4}$ of dressing mixture and toss to combine. If needed, add more dressing, 1 teaspoon at a time, until desired consistency is achieved. Taste and adjust seasoning as desired. Refrigerate until ready to serve. Garnish with fresh cilantro leaves.

Tuna Salad Niçoise

▶ SERVES 4

2 (8-ounce) ahi tuna steaks, cut in half, crosswise
Kosher salt
Lemon pepper
2 tablespoons vegetable oil
1 tablespoon plus 1 teaspoon freshly squeezed lemon juice
1/3 cup olive oil
1/4 cup sherry vinegar
1/4 teaspoon dry mustard
1 teaspoon chopped fresh basil
1/4 cup sliced black olives, drained
1 tablespoon capers, rinsed and drained
3 anchovy fillets, if desired
Fresh lemon wedges, for garnish

1. Pat tuna steaks dry with paper towels. Lightly season with salt and lemon pepper. Heat the vegetable oil in a small heavy-bottomed skillet over high heat until almost smoking. Add tuna steaks and cook until the underside is golden, about 3–4 minutes. Turn steaks and continue to cook until no redness appears in the center. Remove from heat and drizzle 1 tablespoon of lemon juice over the steaks. Let cool to room temperature.

2. Combine the remaining 1 teaspoon of lemon juice, olive oil, vinegar, and dry mustard in a small bowl; whisk until emulsified. Set aside.

3. Transfer tuna steaks to a clean work surface, reserving any accumulated pan juices. Using a fork, flake tuna into large pieces and roughly chop into bite-sized pieces. Transfer chopped tuna and any accumulated pan juices to a medium-sized mixing bowl. Add basil, olives, and capers, and lightly toss. Add half of dressing mixture and toss to combine. If needed, add more dressing, 1 teaspoon at a time, until desired consistency is achieved. Taste and adjust seasoning as desired. Refrigerate until ready to serve. Garnish with anchovy fillets, if using, and lemon wedges.

Three-Bean Salad

▶ YIELDS 6 CUPS

2 cups frozen soybeans
1 (15-ounce) can green beans, drained
1 (15-ounce) can wax beans, drained
¾ cup red wine vinaigrette salad
   dressing
2 tablespoons red wine vinegar
⅓ cup sugar
¼ teaspoon dried tarragon leaves
Dash ground black pepper

CHANGE IT UP

Don't like green beans or don't have them available in your pantry? Use navy beans, cannellini beans, or even black beans.

1. Bring large pot of water to a boil and cook frozen soybeans for 2–3 minutes, until tender. Drain and rinse with cold water. Combine in serving bowl with green beans and wax beans.

2. In small saucepan combine salad dressing, vinegar, sugar, tarragon, and pepper; whisk over low heat until sugar is dissolved. Pour over bean mixture and stir gently. Let stand for 10 minutes, then serve. Store leftovers in refrigerator.

Southwest Potato Salad

▶ SERVES 8

1 quart deli potato salad
1 tablespoon chili powder
2 red bell peppers, chopped

1 pint cherry or grape tomatoes
1 jalapeño pepper, minced
2 cups canned corn, drained

1. Place potato salad in serving bowl and sprinkle evenly with chili powder.

2. Add remaining ingredients and gently stir to mix thoroughly. Serve immediately or cover and chill for 1–2 hours to blend flavors.

Lemon Cucumber Salad

▶ SERVES 6

3 cucumbers

1 teaspoon salt

2 tablespoons plus 1 teaspoon sugar, divided

1 (6-ounce) container lemon-flavored yogurt

$1/3$ cup sour cream

2 tablespoons lemon juice

$1/2$ teaspoon dried thyme leaves

$1/8$ teaspoon white pepper

SUMMER SQUASHES

Summer squashes, like zucchini and yellow squash, are thin-skinned and excellent eaten raw. They can be substituted for cucumbers or mushrooms in most salads. Unless the skins are waxed, they don't need to be peeled, just cut into sticks, julienne, cubes, or slices.

1. Peel cucumbers and slice thinly. Place in colander and sprinkle with salt and 2 tablespoons sugar. Let stand for 15 minutes, then toss cucumbers and press to drain out excess liquid. Rinse cucumbers, drain again, and press between paper towels to dry.

2. Meanwhile, in large bowl, combine yogurt, sour cream, lemon juice, 1 teaspoon sugar, thyme, and pepper and mix well to blend. Gently stir in drained cucumbers, then serve.

Pasta and Cheese Salad

► SERVES 6

1 (10-ounce) container basil pesto
1/2 cup mayonnaise
1 cup cubed smoked Gouda cheese
2 red bell peppers, chopped
1 (18-ounce) package frozen cheese tortellini

1. Bring large pot of salted water to a boil. Meanwhile, in large bowl, combine pesto and mayonnaise and blend well. Stir in cheese and chopped peppers.

2. Add tortellini to pot of water and cook according to package directions until done. Drain well and stir into cheese mixture. Serve immediately or cover and chill for 2–3 hours.

Chicken Tortellini Salad

► SERVES 4-6

1 quart deli tortellini salad
2 cups chopped deli chicken
1 red bell pepper, chopped
1 cup cubed Havarti cheese
1/2 cup mayonnaise

In large bowl, combine all ingredients and toss gently to coat. Serve immediately, or cover and refrigerate up to 24 hours.

SALAD INSPIRATIONS

Take some time to browse through your supermarket to find ideas for salads. In the produce section you'll find salad kits and lots of refrigerated dressings to inspire you. Many companies make salad kits that are placed in the meat aisle, and some are in the grocery aisle near the bottled salad dressings.

Taco Salad

1 pound ground beef
1 (1-ounce) package taco seasoning mix
2 tablespoons vegetable oil
1 small onion, peeled and chopped
1 (16-ounce) can seasoned refried beans
2 (10-ounce) bags mixed salad greens
3 cups blue corn tortilla chips
2 cups shredded Colby cheese

1. In a large skillet, cook ground beef with taco seasoning mix according to package directions. Pour ground beef mixture into a large bowl.

2. In the same skillet, heat oil over medium heat. Cook onion, stirring frequently, until tender, about 5–6 minutes. Stir in refried beans and cook for 3–4 minutes longer, until hot. Combine refried bean mixture with ground beef mixture and set aside.

3. Place salad greens on plates and top with tortilla chips.

4. Spoon beef mixture over tortilla chips and top with shredded cheese. Serve immediately.

Mandarin Orange Salad

▶ SERVES 4

¼ teaspoon black pepper

¼ teaspoon salt

1 cup low-fat cottage cheese

¼ cup reserved mandarin orange juice

1 teaspoon sugar

1 head romaine lettuce leaves, washed, drained, torn

2 green onions, finely chopped

½ medium red onion, peeled and chopped

2 (10-ounce) cans mandarin oranges, drained

MAKE-AHEAD SALADS

Many of the vegetables found in a typical salad, including lettuce, can be prepared ahead of time. Wrap the cut vegetables in paper towels and store in a resealable plastic bag in the crisper section of your refrigerator until ready to use.

1. In a medium bowl, stir pepper and salt into cottage cheese. Stir in mandarin orange juice and sugar.

2. Put torn romaine lettuce leaves in a salad bowl. Toss with onions.

3. Add cottage cheese and mandarin oranges on top.

4. Serve immediately, or chill until ready to serve.

Boiled Egg Salad

2–4 minced Thai chilies

2 tablespoons chopped pickled garlic

3 tablespoons lime juice

1 teaspoon salt

5 large eggs, hard-boiled and sliced lengthwise

2 medium shallots, peeled and thinly sliced, about ¼ cup

¼ cup julienned green apple

¼ cup spearmint

1 medium green onion, trimmed and chopped into 2"-long pieces
    (use both white and green parts)

1. Make dressing by mixing Thai chilies, pickled garlic, lime juice, and salt in a bowl.

2. Place pieces of sliced boiled eggs on a platter. Top with shallots, green apple, spearmint, and green onion.

3. Drizzle dressing on top of the salad and serve at room temperature.

Mango Salad

▶ MAKES 3 CUPS

2 cups julienned green mangoes, 4" long

¼ cup thinly sliced shallot or red onion

¼ cup any kind of chopped, toasted, or fried nuts

2 tablespoons chopped cilantro

3 tablespoons lime juice (more if using cucumbers or carrots)

3 tablespoons fish sauce

2 minced Thai chilies

1 teaspoon sugar

Place everything in a bowl and toss. Adjust to desired taste.

Tuna Salad with Toasted Pine Nuts

▶ SERVES 6

1 (5-ounce) can tuna packed in olive oil, drained and flaked
1 medium shallot, peeled and diced
3 tablespoons chopped fresh chives
1 tablespoon chopped fresh tarragon
1 stalk celery, finely diced
2–3 tablespoons mayonnaise, depending on your preference
1 teaspoon Dijon mustard
$\frac{1}{4}$ teaspoon salt
$\frac{1}{8}$ teaspoon ground black pepper
$\frac{1}{4}$ cup toasted pine nuts

1. In a medium bowl, toss tuna, shallot, chives, tarragon, and celery.
2. In a small bowl, combine mayonnaise, mustard, salt, and pepper. Stir mayonnaise mixture into tuna mixture.
3. Stir in pine nuts. Refrigerate or serve at room temperature.

Strawberry and Feta Salad

▶ SERVES 4

1 teaspoon Dijon mustard
2 tablespoons balsamic vinegar
1 clove garlic, peeled and minced
$\frac{1}{4}$ cup extra-virgin olive oil
$\frac{1}{2}$ teaspoon salt
$\frac{1}{8}$ teaspoon ground black pepper
4 cups salad greens, rinsed and dried
1 pint ripe strawberries, hulled and halved
$1\frac{1}{2}$ cups crumbled feta cheese

1. In a small bowl, whisk mustard, vinegar, garlic, oil, salt, and pepper to make the dressing.
2. In a large bowl, combine salad greens and dressing. Transfer salad to a serving platter and top with the strawberries and feta.
3. Drizzle any remaining dressing over the salad and serve.

Creamy Coleslaw

▶ SERVES 12

1 tablespoon sugar

2 teaspoons salt, divided

¼ cup red wine vinegar

½ large head cabbage, cored and thinly sliced

1 large carrot, peeled and grated

2 green onions, ends trimmed, thinly sliced

2 cloves garlic, peeled and minced

½ cup extra-virgin olive oil

¼ cup mayonnaise

½ cup plain Greek yogurt

½ teaspoon ground black pepper

1. In a large bowl, whisk together sugar, 1½ teaspoons salt, and vinegar. Add cabbage, carrots, green onions, and garlic. Toss to combine. Let vegetables sit 5 minutes.

2. To the vegetables, add oil, mayonnaise, yogurt, pepper, and remaining salt. Stir to combine and coat vegetables in the dressing.

3. Refrigerate or serve at room temperature.

Bean and Olive Salad

▶ SERVES 6

1 cup trimmed green beans

1 large red onion, peeled and thinly
  sliced

2 tablespoons chopped fresh marjoram

¼ cup Kalamata olives, pitted and
  roughly chopped

½ cup cooked red kidney beans

½ cup cooked chickpeas or cannellini
  beans

2 tablespoons extra-virgin olive oil

½ cup balsamic vinegar

1 teaspoon ground black pepper

GREEN VEGETABLES

To maintain the vibrant colors of green vegetables when cooking, make sure not to overcook them. Boil the vegetables al dente and then either serve immediately or shock in ice water and drain.

1. Have large bowl of ice water ready.

2. Bring 1 quart of water to a boil in a large stockpot. Blanch green beans in boiling water 2 minutes, then immediately drain in a colander and shock in ice-water bath. Drain thoroughly.

3. Mix together all ingredients in a large bowl. Refrigerate or serve at room temperature.

Creamy Feta Dressing

 SERVES 8

$1/3$ cup crumbled feta cheese

2 teaspoons water

$3/4$ cup plain yogurt

2 tablespoons mayonnaise

2 tablespoons evaporated milk

1 teaspoon dried oregano

1 clove garlic, peeled and minced

2 tablespoons chopped fresh chives

$1/8$ teaspoon ground black pepper

1. Place feta and water in a medium bowl. Using a fork, mash into a paste.

2. Add remaining ingredients and mix until well incorporated. Keep dressing refrigerated until needed.

Sun-Dried Tomato Vinaigrette

 MAKES ⅔ CUP

$1/3$ cup sun-dried tomatoes, packed in olive oil, rinsed and finely chopped

2 tablespoons balsamic vinegar

1 teaspoon garlic powder

1 teaspoon dried oregano

$1/4$ teaspoon ground black pepper

$1/2$ teaspoon salt

$1/3$ cup extra-virgin olive oil

1. In a small bowl, whisk all ingredients until well incorporated.

2. Keep dressing refrigerated until needed.

Madras Curry Dressing

1 tablespoon oil
1 small red onion, peeled and finely chopped
2 tablespoons chopped red bell pepper
1 teaspoon finely chopped and seeded jalapeño pepper
2 tablespoons Madras curry powder
1 teaspoon ground coriander
1 teaspoon ground turmeric
¼ teaspoon cayenne pepper (optional)
1 tablespoon raisins, soaked in ½ cup warm water
2 tablespoons lime juice
1 cup mayonnaise
2 tablespoons chopped cilantro
Salt and ground black pepper, to taste

1. In a small skillet, heat oil over medium heat for 1 minute. Add onions, bell pepper, and jalapeño. Cook until onions are translucent, about 2 minutes.

2. Add curry powder, coriander, turmeric, and optional cayenne pepper if desired. Cook 4 minutes more, stirring with a wooden spoon. Some of the spices may stick—this is not a problem. Remove from heat; allow to cool a few minutes.

3. Drain the raisins. In the bowl of a food processor, combine onion mixture and raisins. Pulse until smooth, scraping sides of bowl frequently.

4. Add half of lime juice and the mayonnaise. Pulse to combine, then stir in cilantro. Season with salt, pepper, and remaining lime juice. Can be made up to 1 week in advance and stored in the refrigerator.

Aïoli (Garlic Mayonnaise)

▶ SERVES 8

2 large cloves garlic, peeled and finely
   chopped, or pushed through a press

¼ teaspoon salt

2 large egg yolks

1 teaspoon Dijon mustard

Juice of 1 medium lemon (about ¼ cup),
   divided

1 cup extra-virgin olive oil

ROASTED GARLIC VARIATION

For a sweeter, more mature flavor, wrap one whole head of garlic in tinfoil, roast in a 350°F oven for 1 hour, and squeeze the resulting golden brown paste through a strainer. Substitute this roasted garlic purée for the fresh garlic cloves in the Aïoli recipe.

1. Mash together garlic and salt in a large mixing bowl. Wet a cloth towel, wring it out, fold it in half, and set it onto a work surface (this will hold your bowl steady while you work). Set mixing bowl on towel, and mix in yolks, mustard, and 2 teaspoons of lemon juice.

2. Using a rapid whisking action, very gradually whisk ¼ of the olive oil into yolk mixture. Add a few drops of room-temperature water to help incorporate oil, then repeat with remaining oil, adding it in a slow, steady stream, while whisking vigorously. Season to taste with remaining lemon juice.

Classic French Dressing

 SERVES 6

1 teaspoon seasoned salt
1 teaspoon lemon pepper
1 teaspoon dry mustard
$\frac{1}{8}$ cup freshly squeezed lemon juice
$\frac{1}{8}$ cup cider vinegar
$\frac{3}{4}$ cup olive oil

Combine all ingredients in a glass bowl and whisk to combine. Taste and adjust seasoning as desired. Remix just before serving. Refrigerate any unused portion and bring to room temperature before serving.

Creamy Asian Dressing

 SERVES 6

$\frac{3}{4}$ cup mayonnaise
$\frac{1}{4}$ cup sour cream
2 tablespoons tamari sauce (or soy sauce)
1 teaspoon minced garlic
2 tablespoons rice wine
1 teaspoon honey
$\frac{1}{4}$ cup thinly sliced green onion
Freshly ground black pepper, to taste

Combine all ingredients in a nonreactive bowl and whisk until well blended. Taste and adjust seasoning as desired. Refrigerate until ready to use.

SOUPS AND STEWS

Cheddar Cheese Soup

▶ SERVES 4

2 tablespoons butter
$\frac{1}{4}$ cup chopped yellow onion
$\frac{1}{2}$ cup chopped celery
2 tablespoons all-purpose flour
$\frac{1}{2}$ teaspoon ground cayenne pepper
$\frac{1}{4}$ teaspoon dry mustard
$\frac{1}{2}$ tablespoon Worcestershire sauce
1 cup whole milk
$1\frac{1}{2}$ cups chicken stock
2 cups shredded Cheddar cheese
Seasoned salt, to taste
Freshly ground black pepper, to taste
Paprika, for garnish

1. Melt butter in a medium-sized saucepan and sauté onion and celery until tender, about 4 minutes. Add flour, pepper, mustard, and Worcestershire, and mix to combine.

2. Add milk and chicken stock and bring to a boil. Cook for 1 minute, stirring constantly. Reduce heat to low, add cheese, and stir occasionally just until cheese is melted.

3. Add seasoned salt and pepper to taste. To serve, ladle hot soup into small decorative cups and sprinkle with paprika.

Cream of Spinach Soup

 SERVES 6

2 (10-ounce) packages frozen chopped spinach
1 cup chopped white onion
6 cups chicken stock
¼ teaspoon salt
Freshly ground black pepper, to taste
Freshly grated nutmeg, to taste
2 cups half-and-half, at room temperature

1. Combine spinach, onions, and stock in a large saucepan over medium-high heat. Bring to a low boil and reduce heat to a simmer. Cook until spinach is tender, about 10 minutes, stirring occasionally. Remove from heat, add salt, pepper, and nutmeg, and let cool for several minutes.

2. Transfer spinach mixture to a food processor fitted with a metal blade (or a blender). Process until smooth. Work in batches if necessary.

3. Transfer spinach mixture back to the saucepan and slowly add half-and-half, stirring constantly to combine. Reheat gently until heated throughout, about 6–8 minutes; do not boil. Taste and adjust seasoning as desired. Serve hot.

Creamy Broccoli Soup

▶ SERVES 4

1½ pounds broccoli
¾ cup chopped celery
½ cup chopped yellow onion
Salt
2 tablespoons butter
2 tablespoons all-purpose flour
2½ cups chicken stock
⅛ teaspoon freshly grated nutmeg
Freshly ground black pepper, to taste
½ cup heavy cream, at room temperature
½ cup shredded Cheddar cheese, for garnish

1. Trim woody stalks from the broccoli and chop remaining tender stems and tops into medium dice. Combine broccoli, celery, and onions in a medium-sized saucepan. Add just enough water to cover vegetables, and salt generously. Bring to a boil and cook until vegetables are tender but not mushy, about 8 minutes.

2. Use a slotted spoon to transfer vegetables to a food processor fitted with a metal blade (or a blender). Process until smooth, adding a few tablespoons of cooking liquid if needed.

3. Melt butter in a medium-sized saucepan over medium heat. Add flour and whisk until smooth. Cook until smooth and bubbly, about 4 minutes. Slowly add chicken stock, whisking constantly. Bring to a simmer and cook for 2 minutes until thick.

4. Stir in broccoli purée, nutmeg, and salt and pepper to taste; bring to a simmer and cook to allow the flavors to blend. Slowly pour in cream, whisking to blend. Heat through but do not boil. Taste and adjust seasoning as desired. To serve, ladle soup into bowl and top with shredded cheese. Serve hot.

English Garden Pea Soup

▶ SERVES 2

1 tablespoon olive oil
2 cloves garlic, peeled and thinly sliced
1 medium leek, thinly sliced
2 cups garden peas
1 cup white wine
3 tablespoons plain yogurt
3 tablespoons heavy cream, optional
Salt and freshly ground black pepper,
    to taste
Snipped chives
Garlic croutons
Soy bacon (or regular), fried and
    crumbled
Tarragon leaves

RINSING LEEKS

Because leeks are grown in mounds of soil or sand, the grains of which seem to trickle freely between its tightly furled leaves in the stalk, leeks are notoriously gritty and require a thorough rinsing in cold water. One way to get rid of the sand is to slice from just above the root end (leave the root intact for this) and, using a very sharp knife, slit the leek in half lengthwise. Then swish the leek and its separated leaves through a sink of water. When the sand is gone, slice off the root and use.

1. Heat olive oil in a saucepan over medium heat and sauté garlic and leek for 3–4 minutes.

2. Spoon this mixture into a blender or food processor. Add peas, white wine, yogurt, and heavy cream if using. Purée until smooth. Season with salt and pepper.

3. Pour into soup bowls and garnish with chives, croutons, bacon, and tarragon leaves.

Home on the Range Soup

▶ SERVES 4

1 tablespoon vegetable oil
1 pound lean ground beef
1 cup chopped yellow onion
½ cup chopped carrot
⅛ teaspoon garlic salt
Freshly ground black pepper, to taste
¼ cup chickpeas
3 cups beef stock
1 cup salsa (spiciness to taste)
¼ cup sour cream

1. Heat oil in a large heavy-bottomed saucepan over medium-high heat. Add ground beef, onion, and carrot; cook until meat is browned, about 7 minutes, stirring frequently. Break up larger pieces of meat while cooking. Season with garlic salt and pepper.

2. Add chickpeas, stock, and salsa, and bring to a simmer. Cook for 2–3 minutes. To serve, ladle the soup in shallow bowls and top with a dollop of sour cream.

Red Bean and Pasta Soup

▶ SERVES 8

1 medium onion, peeled and chopped

3 cloves garlic, peeled and sliced

3 tablespoons olive oil

1 teaspoon dried oregano

2 bay leaves

1 (8-ounce) can tomato sauce

2 teaspoons salt

1 tablespoon soy sauce

1 (16-ounce) package red beans, soaked overnight in 1 quart cold water
and drained

10 sprigs Italian parsley, including stems

6 cups vegetable stock or water

2 cups cooked pasta (any small shape, such as orzo or ditalini)

1. In a pot large enough to hold all ingredients, cook onions and garlic with olive oil over medium heat for 5 minutes, until onions are translucent. Add oregano, bay leaves, tomato sauce, salt, and soy sauce. Bring to a simmer and add beans, parsley, and stock (or water).

2. Bring to a boil, then reduce to a low simmer and cook for 90 minutes, until beans are tender enough to mash between two fingers.

3. In a blender, purée ⅓ of the beans very well; add them back to the soup. Add cooked pasta, and bring back to a boil for 1 minute more before serving.

Potato Soup

4 slices bacon

1 onion, peeled and chopped

1 (5-ounce) package cheese scalloped
   potato mix

3 cups water

1 (15-ounce) can evaporated milk

2 cups frozen hash brown potatoes

$1/2$ teaspoon dried dill weed

$1/8$ teaspoon white pepper

PRECOOKED BACON?

When recipes call for crumbled bacon, you can use the precooked version. But if the recipe calls for cooking the bacon and using the bacon fat to sauté other ingredients, you must used uncooked bacon. Or you can use the precooked bacon and use butter or olive oil as a substitute for the bacon fat.

1. In heavy saucepan, cook bacon until crisp. Remove bacon, drain on paper towels, crumble, and set aside.

2. Cook onion in bacon drippings until tender, about 5 minutes. Add scalloped potato mix and seasoning packet from potato mix along with remaining ingredients.

3. Bring to a boil and simmer for 17–20 minutes, until potatoes are tender. If desired, purée using an immersion blender. Sprinkle with bacon and serve.

Leek and Potato Soup

$1/4$ cup extra-virgin olive oil

3 medium leeks, trimmed, cleaned, cut lengthwise, and sliced

2 bay leaves

1 teaspoon dried thyme

3 large russet potatoes, peeled and grated

8 cups chicken or vegetable stock

$1/2$ cup heavy cream or evaporated milk

$2^1/2$ teaspoons salt

1 teaspoon ground black pepper

$1/2$ cup chopped fresh chives

1. Add oil to a large pot over medium heat and heat 30 seconds. Add leeks, bay leaves, and thyme. Cook 10–15 minutes or until leeks soften.

2. Add potatoes and cook another 5 minutes. If mixture gets dry or gluey, add some water or stock.

3. Add stock and increase heat to medium-high. Bring soup to a boil, reduce heat to medium-low, and cook 30–40 minutes. Remove bay leaves.

4. Using an immersion blender or a regular blender, carefully purée soup until it is smooth. Add cream, salt, and pepper.

5. Serve hot and topped with chives.

Tomato Bisque

▶ SERVES 6

1 tablespoon olive oil
1 onion, finely chopped
1 (10-ounce) container refrigerated Alfredo sauce
$1\frac{1}{2}$ cups chicken or vegetable broth
$1\frac{1}{2}$ cups whole milk
2 (14-ounce) cans diced tomatoes, undrained
$\frac{1}{2}$ teaspoon dried basil leaves
$\frac{1}{4}$ teaspoon dried marjoram leaves

1. In heavy saucepan, heat olive oil over medium heat and add onion. Cook and stir until onion is tender, about 4 minutes. Add Alfredo sauce and chicken broth; cook and stir with wire whisk until mixture is smooth. Add milk and stir; cook over medium heat for 2–3 minutes.

2. Meanwhile, purée undrained tomatoes in food processor or blender until smooth. Add to saucepan along with seasonings and stir well. Heat soup over medium heat, stirring frequently, until mixture just comes to a simmer. Serve immediately.

Tortellini Soup

▶ SERVES 6–8

1 pound sweet Italian bulk sausage

1 (8-ounce) package sliced mushrooms

4 cloves garlic, peeled and minced

3 (14-ounce) cans beef broth

1½ cups water

1 teaspoon dried Italian seasoning

⅛ teaspoon ground black pepper

1 (24-ounce) package frozen cheese tortellini

FROZEN OR REFRIGERATED TORTELLINI?

Refrigerated, or fresh, tortellini is found in the dairy aisle of the regular grocery store. It is generally more expensive than the frozen, and package sizes are smaller. Frozen tortellini takes a bit longer to cook. Choose your favorite and stock up.

1. In large saucepan over medium heat, brown sausage with mushrooms and garlic, stirring to break up sausage. When sausage is cooked, drain thoroughly. Add broth, water, Italian seasoning, and pepper to saucepan and bring to a boil over high heat. Reduce heat to low and simmer for 8–10 minutes.

2. Stir in frozen tortellini and cook, stirring frequently, over medium-high heat for 6–8 minutes or until tortellini are hot and tender. Serve immediately.

Egg Drop Soup

▶ SERVES 4

4 cups chicken broth or stock
$\frac{1}{8}$ teaspoon ground white pepper
$\frac{1}{4}$ teaspoon salt
$\frac{1}{4}$ teaspoon sugar
1 teaspoon Chinese rice wine or dry sherry
2 large eggs, lightly beaten
2 medium green onions, trimmed and minced
3–4 drops sesame oil

1. Bring chicken stock or broth to a boil.
2. When broth is boiling, add white pepper, salt, sugar, and rice wine. Cook for another minute.
3. Turn off heat and pour eggs into the soup in a steady stream, stirring rapidly in a clockwise direction until they form thin strands.
4. Add green onions and sesame oil. Give the soup a final stir. Serve hot.

Classic Minestrone

▶ SERVES 12

3 tablespoons olive oil

1 cup minced onion

3 stalks celery, chopped

4 cloves garlic, peeled and minced

1 small zucchini, trimmed and chopped

4 cups vegetable broth

2 (14-ounce) cans diced tomatoes, drained

2 (15-ounce) cans red kidney beans, drained

2 (15-ounce) cans cannellini (white) beans, drained

1 (28-ounce) can Italian-style green beans

$\frac{1}{2}$ cup julienned carrots

1 cup red wine (Chianti or Cabernet Sauvignon)

2 (6-ounce) cans tomato paste

2 tablespoons minced parsley

$1\frac{1}{2}$ teaspoons dried oregano

2 teaspoons salt

$\frac{1}{2}$ teaspoon ground black pepper

1 teaspoon garlic powder

$\frac{1}{2}$ teaspoon Italian seasoning

4 cups baby spinach

1 cup cooked small pasta

1. In a large skillet, heat oil over medium heat. Sauté onion, celery, garlic, and zucchini 3–5 minutes until onion is translucent.

2. Add sautéed vegetables and vegetable broth to a 6-quart slow cooker, along with tomatoes, red and white beans, green beans, carrots, wine, tomato paste, parsley, oregano, salt, pepper, garlic powder, and Italian seasoning. Cover and cook on high 8 hours.

3. One hour prior to serving, stir in spinach. When soup is finished, pour into soup bowls and add 1 tablespoon cooked pasta to each bowl.

Cream of Carrot Soup

8 large carrots, scraped and thinly sliced
2 celery stalks, chopped finely
3 cups chicken or vegetable stock
Salt and pepper to taste
1 small bay leaf
1 large egg yolk, beaten
$\frac{1}{4}$ cup heavy whipping cream
$\frac{1}{2}$ cup 2% reduced-fat milk

1. In a large saucepan, combine carrots, celery, stock, salt and pepper, and bay leaf.
2. Bring to a boil and then simmer until carrots are tender, about 10–20 minutes.
3. Discard bay leaf. Pour soup mixture into a blender or food processor and purée until smooth. Return to saucepan and bring to a boil.
4. In a medium bowl combine beaten egg, cream, and milk. Mix a little of the soup with the egg/milk mixture, and then add that mixture to the soup.
5. Stir and bring to a boil for 1 minute. Serve hot or cold.

Chicken Noodle Soup

▶ SERVES 4

3 cups water

1 (3-ounce) package chicken-flavored ramen noodles

1 cup frozen peas

1 cup canned chicken

1 tablespoon soy sauce

$\frac{1}{4}$ teaspoon red pepper flakes

1. Bring water to a boil in a large saucepan over medium-high heat. Add ramen noodles and the contents of flavor packet. Return to a boil, stirring.

2. Add frozen peas. Return to a boil, reduce the heat, and simmer 2–3 minutes, until peas are cooked.

3. Add canned chicken. Stir in soy sauce and red pepper flakes.

4. Return to a boil; then reduce the heat and simmer for 5 more minutes. Serve hot.

Lemony Chicken Soup

 SERVES 4–6

$^1/_2$ cup lemon slices, including peel

3 tablespoons fish sauce

$1^1/_2$ teaspoons chopped hot chili pepper

2 medium green onions, trimmed and thinly sliced

$1^1/_2$ teaspoons sugar

$1^1/_2$ cups coconut milk

2 cups chicken broth

3 teaspoons chopped lemongrass

1 cup straw mushrooms

1 tablespoon minced fresh ginger

1 whole boneless, skinless chicken breast, poached and shredded

1. Combine lemon slices, fish sauce, chili pepper, green onion, and sugar in a small glass bowl; set aside.

2. Combine coconut milk, chicken broth, lemongrass, mushrooms, and ginger in a saucepan. Bring to a boil, reduce heat, and simmer for 20–25 minutes. Add chicken and lemon mixture; heat through.

3. To serve, ladle into warmed bowls.

Chicken Corn Chowder

▶ SERVES 6

1 (26-ounce) jar double-Cheddar pasta
    sauce
2 (14-ounce) cans chicken broth
2 (15-ounce) cans corn, drained
2 (9-ounce) packages frozen cooked
    Southwest-style chicken strips
$\frac{1}{2}$ teaspoon dried Italian seasoning
2 cups shredded sharp Cheddar cheese

In large saucepan, combine all ingredients
except cheese and bring to a boil over
medium-high heat. Reduce heat to low,
cover, and simmer for 6–8 minutes, until
chicken is hot. Stir in Cheddar cheese,
remove from heat, and let stand, covered,
for 3–4 minutes. Stir thoroughly and
serve.

FROZEN PRECOOKED CHICKEN

There are lots of varieties of
frozen precooked chicken
in your supermarket's meat
aisle. You can find cooked
grilled chicken, chicken
strips, and chopped
chicken in flavors that
range from Southwest to
plain grilled. Some varieties
come with a sauce; be sure
to read the label to make
sure you're getting what you
want.

French Onion Soup

▶ SERVES 6

2 tablespoons olive oil

2 tablespoons plus ¼ cup softened butter

2 (10-ounce) packages frozen chopped
  onions

2 tablespoons flour

2 (16-ounce) boxes beef stock

6 slices French bread

1½ cups shredded Gruyère cheese

BOXED STOCKS

If your grocery store carries boxed stocks, buy them. These stocks tend to be richer and less salty than canned stocks. If you don't use all of the stock, these boxes come with a flip-top lid so you can close the box and store them in the refrigerator for a couple of weeks.

1. In large saucepan, combine olive oil and 2 tablespoons butter over medium heat until butter is foamy. Add onions; cook over medium heat for 10–12 minutes, stirring frequently, until onions brown around edges. Sprinkle flour over onions; cook and stir for 2–3 minutes.

2. Stir in stock, bring to a simmer, and cook for 10 minutes. Meanwhile, spread French bread slices with remaining ¼ cup butter. In toaster oven, toast the bread until browned and crisp. Sprinkle with cheese and toast for 2–4 minutes, until cheese melts. Divide soup among soup bowls and float the toasted cheese bread on top.

Beef Burgundy Stew

▶ SERVES 2

1 tablespoon vegetable oil
2 baby onions, cut in half
4 ounces sliced fresh mushrooms
1 zucchini, thinly sliced
$\frac{1}{4}$ teaspoon dried oregano
2 cups leftover cooked beef, cubed
$\frac{1}{4}$ cup Burgundy wine
$\frac{1}{2}$ cup beef broth
1 tablespoon tomato paste
1 tablespoon Worcestershire sauce
$\frac{1}{8}$ teaspoon ground black pepper

1. Heat oil in a skillet on medium heat. Add onions, mushrooms, and zucchini. Stir in dried oregano. Sauté for about 5 minutes, until vegetables are softened.

2. Add beef. Cook for 2–3 minutes to heat through.

3. Add Burgundy wine and beef broth. Stir in tomato paste and Worcestershire sauce. Bring to a boil.

4. Stir in pepper. Turn down the heat and simmer for about 5 minutes. Serve hot.

Mexican Beef Stew

SERVES 6

2 tablespoons olive oil

1 onion, peeled and chopped

1 (16-ounce) package cooked ground
    beef in taco sauce

2 (15-ounce) cans chili beans, undrained

2 cups frozen corn

1 (14-ounce) can Mexican-flavored
    chopped tomatoes, undrained

2 cups water

1 tablespoon chili powder

$\frac{1}{2}$ teaspoon cumin

$\frac{1}{8}$ teaspoon cayenne pepper

SPICES

Spices have a shelf life of
about a year; after that time,
they lose flavor and intensity
and should be replaced.
To keep track, write the
purchase date on the can
or bottle, using a permanent
marker. Periodically, go
through your spice drawer
or rack and discard older
spices; be sure to write
the ones you need on your
grocery list.

In large saucepan, heat olive oil over
medium heat. Add onion; cook and stir
until crisp-tender, about 3–4 minutes.
Add remaining ingredients and stir well. Bring to a simmer, reduce heat to
medium-low, and cook for 10–15 minutes, until corn is hot and soup has
thickened slightly. Serve immediately.

Spanish Beef Stew

Nonstick olive oil cooking spray

1 tablespoon olive oil

2 cloves garlic, peeled and sliced

1 medium onion, peeled and sliced

3 slices bacon, cut into 1" pieces

1 pound stew beef, cubed

3 large Roma tomatoes, diced

1 bay leaf, crumbled

$\frac{1}{4}$ teaspoon dried sage

$\frac{1}{4}$ teaspoon dried marjoram

$\frac{1}{2}$ teaspoon paprika

$\frac{1}{2}$ teaspoon curry powder

1 teaspoon salt

2 tablespoons vinegar

1 cup beef stock

$\frac{1}{2}$ cup white wine

4 medium potatoes, peeled and sliced

$\frac{1}{3}$ cup pitted, sliced olives

2 tablespoons chopped parsley

1. Spray a 4- to 5-quart slow cooker with cooking spray.

2. Heat oil in a large skillet over medium heat. Sauté garlic, onion, bacon, and beef until bacon and beef are done and onion is softened, about 7–8 minutes. Drain and transfer meat mixture to slow cooker.

3. Add tomatoes, bay leaf, sage, marjoram, paprika, curry powder, salt, vinegar, stock, and wine to slow cooker. Cover and cook on low 5 hours.

4. Add potatoes, olives, and parsley to slow cooker and cook 1 hour more.

Beef Stew

▶ SERVES 8

2 pounds bottom-round steak

3 tablespoons flour

$\frac{1}{2}$ teaspoon garlic salt

$\frac{1}{8}$ teaspoon pepper

3 tablespoons olive oil

3 russet potatoes, cubed

1 (16-ounce) package baby carrots

$\frac{1}{2}$ teaspoon dried thyme leaves

$\frac{1}{2}$ teaspoon dried oregano leaves

4 cups beef stock, heated

1 (14-ounce) can diced tomatoes with garlic, undrained

BABY CARROTS

Baby carrots are actually large carrots that have been carefully trimmed and shaped. They are sweeter than the carrots you remember from your childhood because they are a different variety that is bred to grow faster, longer, and with a higher sugar content.

1. Cut steak into 1" cubes. Sprinkle meat with flour, garlic salt, and pepper and toss to coat. Heat oil in the pressure cooker and brown the coated beef, stirring frequently, about 5–7 minutes. Add remaining ingredients and lock the lid. Cook over low heat for 1 hour or until beef is tender.

2. Release pressure using quick-release method and stir stew. Serve immediately.

Mediterranean Stew

▶ SERVES 4

3 tablespoons olive oil

3 cloves garlic, peeled, crushed, and minced

1 (15.5-ounce) can chickpeas, drained and rinsed

1 (19-ounce) can cannellini beans, drained and rinsed

2 cups roasted tomatoes

1½ cups artichoke hearts, quartered

1 cup vegetable broth

4 tablespoons grated Parmesan cheese

1 teaspoon red pepper flakes, or to taste

1 teaspoon dried oregano

Salt and freshly ground black pepper, to taste

Chopped sun-dried tomatoes, for garnish

Chopped Italian parsley, for garnish

Garlic-seasoned croutons, for garnish

Crumbled feta cheese, for garnish

Fresh oregano leaves, for garnish

FETA CHEESE

Feta cheese usually comes cut into small blocks and packed in a brine solution. You can find several different varieties of flavored cheese, including garlic and herbs, sun-dried tomato, plain, peppercorn, basil and tomato, and low fat. Don't drain the brine before you use the cheese, because it helps preserve the cheese.

1. Heat olive oil in a large saucepan over medium heat and sauté the garlic for 2–3 minutes or until golden.

2. Reduce heat to medium-low. Stir in chickpeas, cannellini beans, roasted tomatoes, artichoke hearts, broth, Parmesan cheese, red pepper flakes, oregano, salt, and pepper. Cook and stir for about 10 minutes.

3. Serve in individual bowls, garnishing with sun-dried tomatoes, parsley, croutons, feta, and oregano.

Asian Pork Stew

▶ SERVES 4

2 tablespoons all-purpose flour

2 teaspoons Chinese five-spice powder

1$\frac{1}{2}$ pounds pork tenderloin, trimmed of excess fat and cut into $\frac{3}{4}$" cubes

2 tablespoons olive oil

1 cup sliced celery

$\frac{3}{4}$ cup sliced red onion

$\frac{1}{2}$ cup large-diced green peppers

1 tablespoon minced garlic

1 cup chicken stock

2 tablespoons hoisin sauce

2 tablespoons tamari

$\frac{1}{2}$ teaspoon ground ginger

8 ounces zucchini, cut into $\frac{1}{4}$"-thick rounds and halved

3 tablespoons toasted sesame seeds, for garnish

Fresh cilantro leaves, for garnish

1. Combine flour and five-spice powder in a shallow bowl. Dredge pork pieces in flour and shake off excess, reserving excess flour.

2. Heat 1 tablespoon of oil in a large nonstick skillet over medium-high heat. Add pork and brown on all sides, stirring occasionally to cook evenly, about 6 minutes. Use a slotted spoon to transfer meat to a plate and tent with tinfoil to keep warm.

3. Add remaining tablespoon of oil and celery, onions, peppers, and garlic. Cook until soft, about 4 minutes, stirring occasionally. Return pork to pan and add stock, hoisin, tamari, ginger, and zucchini. Bring to a simmer and cook until vegetables are crisp-tender and meat is tender and cooked through, about 18 minutes.

4. Add 3–4 tablespoons of pan juices to reserved flour and whisk until there are no lumps. Add flour mixture to stew and whisk to combine. Cook and stir until thick. To serve, ladle stew into warm shallow soup bowls and garnish with sesame seeds and cilantro leaves.

Tuscan Chicken and Sausage Stew

▶ SERVES 4–6

Nonstick olive oil cooking spray
1 pound boneless, skinless chicken thighs, cut into bite-sized pieces
8 ounces turkey sausage, cut into $1/2$" slices
1 (26-ounce) jar pasta sauce
1 (14.5-ounce) can green beans, drained
1 teaspoon dried oregano

1. Spray a 4- to 5-quart slow cooker with cooking spray.
2. Place all ingredients in slow cooker and stir to combine. Cook on high 4 hours or on low 8 hours.

Jamaican Red Bean Stew

▶ SERVES 4

2 tablespoons olive oil
$1/2$ medium onion, diced
2 cloves garlic, peeled and minced
1 (15-ounce) can diced tomatoes
3 cups sweet potatoes, peeled and diced
2 (15-ounce) cans red kidney beans, drained
1 cup coconut milk
3 cups vegetable broth
2 teaspoons jerk seasoning
2 teaspoons curry powder
Salt and pepper, to taste

1. In a sauté pan over medium heat, add the olive oil, then sauté the onion and garlic for about 3 minutes.
2. In a 4-quart slow cooker, add all ingredients. Cover and cook on low heat for 6 hours.

Two-Bean Chili

▶ SERVES 4

2 tablespoons olive oil

1 onion, chopped

1 (1.25-ounce) package taco seasoning
  mix

1 (15-ounce) can kidney beans, drained

1 (15-ounce) can black beans, drained

2 (14-ounce) cans diced tomatoes with
  green chilies, undrained

1 cup water

TACO SEASONING MIX

You can make your own taco seasoning mix by combining 2 tablespoons chili powder, 2 teaspoons onion powder, 2 tablespoons cornstarch, 1 teaspoon dried oregano, 1 teaspoon dried red pepper flakes, 2 teaspoons salt, and ½ teaspoon cumin. Blend well and store in a cool dry place: 2 tablespoons equals one envelope mix.

1. In heavy saucepan over medium heat, add olive oil and sauté onion until tender, about 4–5 minutes. Sprinkle taco seasoning mix over onions; cook and stir for 1 minute. Add drained but not rinsed beans, tomatoes, and water.

2. Bring to a simmer; cook for 10–12 minutes, until thickened and blended.

Five-Ingredient Chili

SERVES 4-6

1½ pounds ground beef

1 onion, chopped

2 tablespoons flour

1 (4-ounce) can chopped jalapeños, undrained

2 (8-ounce) cans tomato sauce with seasonings

2 (14-ounce) cans diced tomatoes with garlic, undrained

1 cup water

FIVE-WAY CHILI

In Cincinnati, "five-way chili" means chili served with spaghetti, Cheddar cheese, beans, and chopped raw onions. If you vary the additions, you'll be serving "two-way" (with spaghetti), "three-way" (spaghetti and cheese), and "four-way" (three-way plus raw onions). "One-way," of course, is plain chili.

1. In large saucepan, cook ground beef and onion over medium heat, stirring frequently to break up meat, about 4–5 minutes. When beef is browned, drain off half of the liquid. Sprinkle flour over beef; cook and stir for 2 minutes.

2. Add remaining ingredients, bring to a simmer, and simmer for 10–15 minutes, until flavors are blended and liquid is thickened. Serve immediately.

Vegan Chili

▶ SERVES 8

¼ cup olive oil

2 cups chopped onions

1 cup chopped carrots

2 cups chopped assorted bell peppers

2 teaspoons salt

1 tablespoon chopped garlic

2 small jalapeño peppers, seeded and chopped

1 tablespoon ground ancho chili pepper or ½ teaspoon red pepper flakes

1 chipotle in adobo, chopped

1 tablespoon toasted cumin seeds, ground or 4 teaspoons ground cumin, toasted briefly in a dry pan

1 (28-ounce) can plum tomatoes, roughly chopped, juice included

1 (16-ounce) can red kidney beans, rinsed and drained

1 (16-ounce) can cannellini beans, rinsed and drained

1 (16-ounce) can black beans, rinsed and drained

1 cup tomato juice

Finely chopped red onions, for garnish

Chopped fresh cilantro, for garnish

1. Heat oil in a heavy-bottomed Dutch oven or soup pot. Add onions, carrots, bell peppers, and salt; cook 15 minutes over medium heat, until onions are soft. Add garlic, jalapeños, ancho, chipotle, and cumin; cook 5 minutes more.

2. Stir in tomatoes, beans, and tomato juice. Simmer about 45 minutes. Serve garnished with red onions and cilantro.

BEEF MAIN DISHES

Basic Beef Stir-Fry

▶ SERVES 2–4

2 teaspoons soy sauce

1 teaspoon cornstarch

¼ teaspoon baking soda

½ pound beef, cut into thin strips

1 tablespoon vegetable oil

2 tablespoons oil for stir-frying

1 clove garlic, peeled and smashed

1 tablespoon Chinese rice wine or dry sherry

½ teaspoon sugar

SEARING MEAT

While stir-frying is normally a hands-on process, when cooking meat it's best to give the spatula a brief rest. Lay the meat out flat in the wok and brown for about 30 seconds before stir-frying.

1. In a medium bowl, add soy sauce, cornstarch, and baking soda to the meat, in that order. Use your hands to mix in cornstarch and baking soda. Marinate for 30 minutes. Add vegetable oil. Marinate for another 30 minutes.

2. Add oil to a preheated wok or medium skillet. When oil is hot, add garlic and stir-fry briefly until aromatic. Add beef, laying it flat on the wok. Let the meat cook for a minute, turn over and brown on the other side, and then begin stir-frying. When it is nearly cooked through, add the rice wine and sugar. When the meat is cooked, remove from wok and drain on paper towels.

Beef Main Dishes

Ginger Meatball Stir-Fry

▶ SERVES 6

1 (16-ounce) package frozen meatballs

3 tablespoons oil

1 onion, peeled and chopped

2 cloves garlic, peeled and minced

2 (9-ounce) boxes frozen Asian
   vegetables in sesame-ginger sauce

½ cup beef broth

STIR-FRY TIPS

When stir-frying, always make sure the oil is hot before adding the food. Stir vegetables continually to keep them from sticking to the bottom of the pan. When stir-frying meat, allow it to brown briefly before you begin stirring.

1. Place meatballs in a 12" × 8" microwave-safe dish and heat on high power for 4 minutes. Rearrange meatballs and heat on high power for 2 minutes longer. Set aside.

2. In heavy skillet or wok, heat oil over high heat. Add onion and garlic; stir-fry for 4–5 minutes, until onion is crisp-tender. Add frozen vegetables in sauce and beef broth and bring to a boil over high heat. Cover, reduce heat, and simmer for 5 minutes.

3. Uncover pan and add meatballs. Stir-fry for 3–5 minutes longer, until vegetables and meatballs are hot and sauce is slightly thickened. Serve immediately.

Beef Tacos

SERVES 4–6

1 (16-ounce) package cooked ground
    beef in taco sauce
2 tablespoons olive oil
1 onion, peeled and chopped
1 (15-ounce) can seasoned refried beans
12 crisp taco shells
2 cups shredded Co-Jack cheese

1. Preheat oven to 400°F. Heat beef
and sauce according to package
directions. Meanwhile, heat olive oil
in large skillet over medium heat.
Cook onion, stirring frequently,
until tender, about 5–6 minutes.
Stir in refried beans and cook for
3–4 minutes longer, until hot.

2. Place taco shells on a baking sheet and heat at 400°F for 4–7 minutes,
until crisp. Serve the ground-beef mixture along with the refried-beans
mixture, the taco shells, and shredded cheese and let diners make their
own tacos.

TACOS: CRISP OR SOFT?

You can make crisp tacos, usually with preformed shells heated in the oven, or soft tacos, made by heating tortillas until softened, then filling and folding to enclose the filling. Soft tacos are essentially the same as burritos, but they aren't fried or baked after filling. Don't worry too much about the nomenclature—just enjoy the food!

Meaty Spaghetti

1 (16-ounce) package cooked meatloaf in
   tomato sauce
2 tablespoons olive oil
1 onion, chopped
1 (28-ounce) jar pasta sauce
1 pound spaghetti
1 cup grated Parmesan cheese

RECIPE SUBSTITUTIONS

You could use leftover meatloaf in this easy spaghetti recipe, or use frozen precooked meatballs, heated according to the package directions, along with 1 (8-ounce) can of tomato sauce. For more nutrition, add some preshredded carrots to the pan when adding the meatloaf and let simmer in the sauce.

1. Bring a large pot of water to a boil over high heat. Remove meatloaf from package and crumble. In heavy saucepan, heat olive oil over medium heat. Cook onion for 4–5 minutes, stirring frequently, until crisp-tender. Add crumbled meatloaf, tomato sauce from package, and pasta sauce. Bring to a simmer; cook for 7–9 minutes, until sauce is slightly thickened.

2. Meanwhile, add spaghetti to boiling water and cook according to package directions, until al dente. Drain well and place on serving platter. Top with meat mixture and sprinkle with Parmesan cheese. Serve immediately.

Mini Meatloaf

▶ SERVES 6

2 large eggs
$\frac{1}{2}$ teaspoon dried Italian seasoning
$\frac{1}{2}$ teaspoon onion salt
$\frac{1}{8}$ teaspoon garlic pepper
$\frac{3}{4}$ cup soft bread crumbs
$\frac{3}{4}$ cup ketchup, divided
$1\frac{1}{2}$ pounds meatloaf mix
1 cup shredded Co-Jack cheese, divided

ABOUT MEATLOAF MIX

Meatloaf mix is found in the meat aisle of the supermarket. It usually consists of one-third beef, one-third pork, and one-third veal, but read the label to find out what the blend is in your area. The veal lightens the mixture, and the pork adds a slightly different flavor and texture, because meatloaf made with all beef tends to be heavy.

1. Preheat oven to 350°F. In large bowl, combine eggs, Italian seasoning, onion salt, garlic pepper, bread crumbs, and $\frac{1}{2}$ cup ketchup and mix well. Add meatloaf mix and $\frac{1}{2}$ cup cheese and mix gently but thoroughly to combine.

2. Press meat mixture, $\frac{1}{3}$ cup at a time, into 12 muffin cups. Top each with a bit of ketchup and remaining cheese. Bake at 350°F for 15–18 minutes, until meat is thoroughly cooked. Remove from muffin tins, drain if necessary, place on serving platter, cover with tinfoil, and let stand 5 minutes before serving.

Quick Beef Stroganoff

▶ SERVES 4

2 tablespoons olive oil

1 onion, chopped

1 (16-ounce) package fully cooked beef tips with gravy

1 (16-ounce) package frozen cut green beans, thawed and drained

4 cups egg noodles

1 cup sour cream

1. Bring a large pot of water to a boil. Meanwhile, heat olive oil in large saucepan over medium heat. Add onion; cook and stir for 3–4 minutes, until crisp-tender. Add contents of beef package along with green beans. Bring to a simmer; cook for 6–7 minutes, until beef and green beans are heated.

2. When water is boiling, add egg noodles. Cook according to package directions, until al dente, about 4–5 minutes. Meanwhile, stir sour cream into beef mixture, cover, and remove from heat. When noodles are done, drain well, place on serving platter, and spoon beef mixture over.

Grilled Steak Kebabs

▶ SERVES 4

1 pound sirloin steak
¾ cup barbecue sauce
2 tablespoons cola beverage
¼ teaspoon garlic pepper
8 ounces cremini mushrooms
2 red bell peppers, cut into strips

1. Cut steak into 1" cubes and combine with barbecue sauce, cola beverage, and garlic pepper in a medium bowl. Massage the marinade into the meat with your hands; let stand for 10 minutes.

2. Meanwhile, prepare vegetables and preheat grill. Thread steak cubes, mushrooms, and bell peppers onto metal skewers and place on grill over medium coals. Grill, covered, brushing frequently with remaining marinade, for 7–10 minutes, turning frequently, until steak reaches desired doneness. Discard any remaining marinade. Serve immediately.

GRILL TEMPERATURES

Check the temperature of your grill by carefully holding your hand about 6" above the coals and counting how many seconds you can hold your hand steady before it gets too hot. If you can hold your hand for 5 seconds, the coals are low; 4 seconds, medium; 3 seconds, medium-high; and 2 seconds, high.

Spicy Flank Steak

▶ SERVES 4-6

3 cloves garlic, peeled
1 teaspoon salt
1 tablespoon grill seasoning
$\frac{1}{4}$ teaspoon dry mustard
$\frac{1}{4}$ teaspoon cayenne pepper
2 tablespoons balsamic vinegar
$1\frac{1}{2}$ pounds flank steak

IT'S ALL IN THE SLICING

Flank steak is a lean, flavorful cut that is tender only if sliced correctly. Look at the steak: you'll see parallel lines running through it. That's called the grain of the steak. When you cut the steak, cut against, or perpendicular to, those lines and the steak will be tender and juicy.

1. On cutting board, mince garlic cloves; then sprinkle with salt. Using the side of the knife, mash garlic and salt together to create a paste. Place in a small bowl and add remaining ingredients except flank steak; mix well.

2. Prick both sides of the steak with a fork and rub the marinade mixture into the steak. Let stand for 10 minutes.

3. Pan-fry the steak for 5 minutes; then turn steak, cover, and fry for 3–5 minutes longer, until medium-rare or medium. Let steak stand for 5 minutes, and then slice across the grain to serve.

Panang Curry with Beef

▶ SERVES 4

2 (13.5-ounce) cans coconut milk (do not shake the cans)
½ cup Panang curry paste
2 pounds sliced beef sirloin
2 tablespoons fish sauce
2 tablespoons sugar
6 torn kaffir lime leaves
1 cup Thai basil

1. Do not shake coconut milk cans. Scoop cream on top of coconut milk, about halfway down. In a large frying pan, bring cream to a boil over medium heat. Stir in curry paste and turn down the heat to low. Simmer over low heat, without stirring, until fragrant and coconut cream starts to release some oil, about 3–5 minutes.

2. Add sliced beef to mixture and simmer for 2 minutes, stirring occasionally. Add rest of coconut milk and bring it back to boil. Simmer beef for 30 minutes at low heat.

3. Season with fish sauce and sugar. Taste for seasoning. Add kaffir lime and Thai basil leaves and turn off heat.

Beef with Peppers

SERVES 6

1½ pounds flank steak, cut across the grain into thin slices

2 tablespoons dark soy sauce

2 tablespoons Chinese rice wine or dry sherry, divided

1 teaspoon sesame oil

1 tablespoon cornstarch

¼ cup water

2 tablespoons soy sauce

1 teaspoon sugar

4½ tablespoons vegetable oil, divided

2 cloves garlic, peeled and chopped

2 slices ginger, chopped

½ medium red bell pepper, seeded and cut into thin strips

½ medium green bell pepper, seeded and cut into thin strips

½ cup canned bamboo shoots, rinsed and drained

WHY CUT MEAT ACROSS THE GRAIN?

The "grains" running across a piece of flank steak are muscle fibers. Since the muscle is the part of the body that does all the work, these fibers are tough. Cutting the meat against—instead of with—the grain shortens the muscle fibers, giving the meat a more tender texture. This technique is not as important with pork and chicken, as that meat is more tender to begin with.

1. Place beef slices in a medium bowl. Mix in dark soy sauce, 1 tablespoon rice wine, sesame oil, and cornstarch, adding the cornstarch last. Marinate beef for 30 minutes. In a small bowl, mix water, 1 tablespoon of rice wine, soy sauce, and sugar. Set aside.

2. Add 3 tablespoons of oil to a preheated wok or medium skillet. Add garlic and ginger and stir-fry briefly until aromatic. Add beef and stir-fry in batches until beef changes color, 3–4 minutes. Remove and set aside.

3. Wipe the wok with a paper towel. Add 1½ tablespoons of oil to the wok. When oil is hot, add red and green peppers. Stir-fry briefly and add bamboo shoots. Add prepared sauce and bring to a boil.

4. Add beef. Mix everything through. Serve hot.

Curried Rice Noodles with Beef

> SERVES 3-4

1 pound flank steak

1½ tablespoons light soy sauce

1 tablespoon Chinese rice wine or dry sherry

¼ teaspoon ground black pepper

2 teaspoons cornstarch

4–5 ounces rice vermicelli noodles

3 tablespoons chicken broth

1 tablespoon dark soy sauce

¾ teaspoon sugar

¼ teaspoon salt

¼ teaspoon chili paste

4 tablespoons vegetable or peanut oil, divided

2 cloves garlic, peeled and minced, divided

2 thin slices ginger, minced, divided

3 tablespoons curry powder

1 medium onion, peeled and chopped

1 medium tomato, cut into thin slices, and each slice cut in half

1 cup mung bean sprouts

1. Cut steak across the grain into thin strips about ½" wide, ⅛" thick, and 1½"–2" long. Place steak in a bowl and add light soy sauce, rice wine or sherry, black pepper, and cornstarch. Marinate steak for 15 minutes.

2. Soak rice noodles in hot water for 15–20 minutes until softened. Drain thoroughly and cut noodles crosswise into thirds. Combine chicken broth, dark soy sauce, sugar, salt, and chili paste in a small bowl.

Curried Rice Noodles with Beef—continued

3. Heat a wok or medium skillet over medium-high heat until nearly smoking and add 2 tablespoons oil. When oil is hot, add half the garlic and ginger. Stir-fry for 10 seconds, then add half the beef. Let meat sear for about 30 seconds before starting to stir-fry, then move meat around quickly with a spatula until it loses any pinkness and is nearly cooked through. Remove and drain in a colander or on paper towels. Repeat with the remainder of beef.

4. Heat 2 tablespoons oil in a wok or medium skillet. When oil is hot, add remaining garlic and ginger and curry powder. Stir-fry for 10 seconds, then add onion. Stir-fry onion, mixing it in with the seasonings, until it begins to soften (about 2 minutes). Add tomato and stir-fry for a minute.

5. Stir in bean sprouts. Stir-fry for about 1 minute, then add beef and noodles. Add chicken broth mixture. Stir-fry for another minute or until noodles have absorbed the chicken broth mixture. Serve hot.

Stir-Fried Orange Beef

▶ SERVES 4–6

2 teaspoons Chinese rice wine or dry
  sherry, divided
$\frac{1}{2}$ teaspoon baking soda
1 pound sirloin or flank steak, shredded
$\frac{1}{3}$ cup dried orange peel, cut into thin
  slices
1 medium green onion, trimmed and cut
  on the diagonal into $1\frac{1}{2}$" slices
2 tablespoons soy sauce
1 teaspoon sugar
$\frac{1}{4}$ teaspoon chili paste
3 tablespoons oil for stir-frying, divided
2 slices ginger, minced
1 clove garlic, peeled and minced

> **ORANGE PEEL COLD CURE**
>
> Have a cold? Why not try an orange peel cure? For centuries, Chinese medical practitioners have recommended dried orange peel to treat everything from colds to insomnia. Whatever their medicinal value, there is no doubt that the peel contains more vitamin C than any other part of the orange.

1. Add 1 teaspoon rice wine and baking soda to a bowl. Add the beef. Marinate for 30 minutes.

2. Cut dried orange peel into thin slices. Cut green onion into $1\frac{1}{2}$" slices on the diagonal.

3. Combine soy sauce, sugar, chili paste, and 1 teaspoon rice wine. Set aside.

4. Add 2 tablespoons oil to a preheated wok or medium skillet. When oil is hot, add beef. Stir-fry until it is nearly cooked through. Remove from the wok and drain on paper towels.

5. Add 1 tablespoon oil. Add ginger, garlic, green onion, and dried orange peel. Stir-fry until orange peel is aromatic. Add the sauce in the middle and bring to a boil. Put beef back in. Mix everything and stir-fry until beef is cooked through. Serve hot.

Hot Hunan Beef

1 pound flank steak, cut into $1\frac{1}{2}$"–2" long strips

1 tablespoon soy sauce

2 tablespoons rice wine or dry sherry, divided

2 teaspoons cornstarch

1 tablespoon dark soy sauce

1 tablespoon white rice vinegar

1 tablespoon water

$1\frac{1}{2}$ teaspoons Asian sesame oil

$\frac{1}{8}$ teaspoon ground white pepper

$3\frac{1}{2}$ tablespoons vegetable or peanut oil, divided

2 teaspoons minced ginger

1 tablespoon minced garlic

1 teaspoon chili paste

1 teaspoon sugar

1. Place beef in a bowl and add soy sauce, 1 tablespoon rice wine or dry sherry, and cornstarch. Marinate for 20 minutes.

2. In a small bowl, combine 1 tablespoon rice wine or dry sherry, dark soy sauce, rice vinegar, water, Asian sesame oil, and white pepper. Set aside.

3. Heat a wok or medium skillet until it is nearly smoking. Add 2 tablespoons oil. When oil is hot, add minced ginger. Stir-fry for 10 seconds, then add half the beef, laying it flat in the pan. Let sear (brown) briefly, then stir-fry, stirring and tossing the meat until it is no longer pink. Remove and drain in a colander or on paper towels.

4. Wipe the pan clean and add $1\frac{1}{2}$ tablespoons oil. When oil is hot, add garlic and chili paste. Stir-fry for about 30 seconds, then add beef back into the pan. Add rice wine-soy sauce mixture. Heat to boiling, stirring to combine the meat with the sauce and chili paste. Stir in the sugar. Serve hot.

Cashew Beef

$^3/_4$ pound top sirloin steak, cut against the grain into thin strips

$1^1/_2$ tablespoons oyster sauce

1 tablespoon soy sauce

$^1/_4$ teaspoon ground black pepper

$1^1/_2$ teaspoons cornstarch

$^1/_2$ cup raw, unsalted cashews

3 tablespoons vegetable or peanut oil, divided

1 teaspoon minced garlic

$^1/_2$ cup canned sliced water chestnuts, drained

$^1/_2$ cup canned sliced bamboo shoots, drained

$^1/_2$ teaspoon salt

1. Place beef in a bowl and add oyster sauce, soy sauce, pepper, and cornstarch. Marinate for 20 minutes.

2. Roast cashews in a large heavy frying pan over medium heat, shaking the pan continuously so that the nuts do not burn. Roast until cashews are browned (about 5 minutes). Remove cashews from pan to cool.

3. Heat a wok or medium skillet over medium-high heat until it is nearly smoking. Add 2 tablespoons oil. When oil is hot, add beef, laying it flat in the pan. Let sear (brown) briefly, then stir-fry the meat, stirring and tossing until it is no longer pink. Remove and drain in a colander or on paper towels.

4. Heat 1 tablespoon oil in the wok or skillet. When oil is hot, add garlic. Stir-fry for 10 seconds, then add water chestnuts, bamboo shoots, and salt. Stir-fry for 1 minute, then add beef. Add cashews. Stir-fry for another minute to combine all ingredients. Serve hot.

Keftedes

2 pounds lean ground beef
2 medium onions, peeled and grated
2 slices bread, soaked in water,
    squeezed dry, and crumbled
1 tablespoon minced garlic
2 large eggs, beaten
2 teaspoons dried oregano
2 tablespoons chopped fresh parsley
1 teaspoon chopped fresh mint
$\frac{1}{8}$ teaspoon ground cumin
$2\frac{1}{2}$ teaspoons salt
$\frac{3}{4}$ teaspoon ground black pepper

GREEK OREGANO

In Greek, *oregano* means "joy of the mountain." Greek oregano has wider and fuzzier leaves than the common variety. When dried, it has an unmistakable and distinct pungent aroma. Whenever possible, use Greek oregano in your dishes.

1. In a large bowl, combine all ingredients and mix well.

2. Use your hands to form 16 (2½") patties with the meat mixture; place them on a tray. Wrap the tray with plastic wrap and refrigerate for at least 4 hours or overnight.

3. Pan-fry the patties over medium-high heat 3–4 minutes per side. Serve immediately.

Meatballs with Mushrooms

▶ SERVES 6

Nonstick olive oil cooking spray

1 pound lean ground beef

1 clove garlic, peeled and minced

$\frac{1}{4}$ cup chopped celery

$\frac{1}{2}$ cup uncooked rice

$\frac{1}{2}$ cup dried bread crumbs

$\frac{1}{2}$ teaspoon dried sage

$\frac{1}{2}$ teaspoon salt

$\frac{1}{2}$ teaspoon ground white pepper

3 tablespoons vegetable oil, divided

$\frac{1}{2}$ pound mushrooms, minced

1 medium onion, peeled and minced

1 tablespoon all-purpose flour

1 cup water

1 cup tomato sauce

RICE AND SLOW COOKING

When making rice in a slow cooker, use converted rice (not instant) and it will come out light and fluffy. You can also add vegetables and spices to the rice for an easy meal.

1. Spray a 4- to 5-quart slow cooker with cooking spray.

2. In a large bowl, combine ground beef, garlic, celery, rice, bread crumbs, sage, salt, and pepper. Form mixture into ¾" balls.

3. Heat 2 tablespoons oil in a large skillet over medium heat. Brown meatballs on all sides, about 1 minute per side, and drain on a paper-towel-lined plate. Arrange meatballs in slow cooker.

4. Heat remaining oil in a skillet over medium-high heat. Sauté mushrooms and onion until softened, about 5 minutes. Add flour to mushroom mixture and stir to thicken. Add water and tomato sauce and mix until smooth.

5. Pour tomato and mushroom mixture over meatballs.

6. Cover and cook on low 3–4 hours.

Paprika Meatballs

▶ SERVES 12

Nonstick olive oil cooking spray
1 pound ground veal
1 pound ground pork
1 clove garlic, peeled and minced
¼ pound shredded mozzarella cheese
3 large eggs
1 tablespoon paprika
1 teaspoon salt
1 cup dried bread crumbs
½ cup 2% milk
2 tablespoons vegetable oil
2 large plum tomatoes, diced
1 cup tomato sauce

PASTA AND SLOW COOKING

Pasta is a great addition to slow-cooked meals, but it shouldn't be added at the beginning of cooking. Add uncooked pasta to the slow cooker about an hour before serving.

1. Spray a 4- to 5-quart slow cooker with cooking spray.

2. Combine veal, pork, garlic, and cheese in a large bowl with eggs, paprika, salt, bread crumbs, and milk; mix well. Form mixture into ¾" balls.

3. Heat oil in a large skillet over medium heat. Brown meatballs on all sides, about 1 minute per side, and drain on a paper-towel-lined plate. Arrange meatballs in slow cooker.

4. Pour tomatoes and tomato sauce over meatballs in slow cooker.

5. Cover and cook on low 3–4 hours.

Albuquerque-Style Salisbury Steak

▶ SERVES 4

1½ pounds ground chuck beef

½ cup shredded pepper jack cheese

¼ cup chopped fresh cilantro

1 (4-ounce) can chopped mild green chilies

2 tablespoons minced green onions

2 teaspoons chili powder

1 teaspoon salt

Freshly ground black pepper, to taste

2 tablespoons vegetable oil

1 cup salsa

MAKE STEAK AHEAD

These steaks can be made a day ahead, wrapped in plastic wrap and refrigerated. Allow the steaks to sit at room temperature for about 15 minutes before cooking for better control of internal temperatures.

1. Combine the beef, cheese, cilantro, chilies, green onions, chili powder, and salt in a medium-sized mixing bowl. Gently combine with a fork or your hands. Compress very lightly into 4 oval patties, about ¾" thick. Sprinkle with pepper.

2. Heat the oil in a nonstick skillet over medium-high heat. Add the steaks and cook until brown on both sides, about 6 minutes per side for medium-rare. Transfer the steaks to a plate and tent with tinfoil to keep warm. Let rest for 4–5 minutes to allow the juices to reabsorb.

3. To serve, place a steak on each serving plate and add a portion of the salsa on the side. Serve hot.

PORK MAIN DISHES

Pork and Apricot Skewers

▶ SERVES 6

1½ pounds boneless pork tenderloin
1 cup apricot preserves
½ cup apricot nectar
12 dried whole apricots
2 onions
½ teaspoon dried thyme leaves

> **KEBABS**
>
> When you're making skewers or kebabs, there are different materials to choose from. Bamboo skewers must be soaked in water for at least 30 minutes before grilling so they won't burn while the food is cooking. Metal skewers are more durable, but use caution because they get very hot when on the grill.

1. Prepare and heat grill. Cut pork into 1" cubes and place in medium bowl. Top with apricot preserves; let stand while preparing remaining ingredients. In small saucepan, combine apricot nectar and dried apricots; bring to a boil over high heat. Reduce heat and simmer for 3 minutes; remove apricots and set on wire rack to cool; pour hot nectar over pork cubes. Cut onions into 6 wedges each.

2. Drain pork, reserving marinade, and thread pork cubes, onion wedges, and apricots onto 6 metal skewers. Combine the reserved marinade with the thyme leaves in a small pan and bring to a boil over medium-high heat; reduce heat to low and simmer while skewers cook.

3. Grill skewers, covered, over medium coals for 5 minutes. Turn and brush with some of the simmering marinade. Cover and grill for 5–8 minutes longer, until pork is slightly pink in center and onions are crisp-tender; keep marinade simmering. Serve with the marinade on the side.

Grilled Orange Pork Tenderloin

SERVES 6-8

2 (1-pound) pork tenderloins

1 teaspoon salt

$\frac{1}{8}$ teaspoon pepper

$\frac{1}{3}$ cup frozen orange juice concentrate, thawed

$\frac{1}{4}$ cup honey

$\frac{1}{4}$ cup Dijon mustard

1 tablespoon lemon juice

$\frac{1}{2}$ teaspoon dried oregano leaves

BUTTERFLYING MEATS

Butterflying meat cuts the cooking time almost in half. You can butterfly just about any cut of meat. Use a sharp knife and cut slowly, being sure not to cut all the way through to the other side. Spread the cut meat out, and if desired, use a meat mallet to gently pound it to flatten to an even thickness.

1. Prepare and heat grill. Cut pork tenderloins in half crosswise. Then butterfly the pork; cut the tenderloins horizontally in half, being careful not to cut through to the other side. Spread tenderloins open and place in large casserole dish. Sprinkle both sides with salt and pepper. In medium bowl, combine remaining ingredients and mix well. Spread on all sides of tenderloins and let stand for 10 minutes.

2. Grill tenderloins, 6" from medium coals, covered, turning once, for 14–17 minutes, until a meat thermometer registers 160°F. Brush with any remaining marinade after turning. Discard remaining marinade. Slice tenderloins across the grain to serve.

Italian Crispy Pork Chops

▶ SERVES 6–8

8 thin-cut boneless pork chops
2 large eggs, beaten
2 tablespoons water
$\frac{1}{2}$ cup grated Parmesan cheese
1 cup panko
1 teaspoon dried Italian seasoning
$\frac{1}{2}$ teaspoon dried basil leaves
2 tablespoons butter
3 tablespoons olive oil

PANKO BREAD CRUMB SUBSTITUTIONS

Panko are Japanese bread crumbs that are very light, dry, and rough. If you can't find them, make your own soft bread crumbs from a fresh loaf of bread, spread them on a baking sheet, and bake them in a 350°F oven for 5–8 minutes, until dry and crisp.

1. Place pork chops between 2 pieces of plastic wrap and pound with a rolling pin or meat mallet until about $\frac{1}{3}$" thick. In shallow bowl, combine eggs and water and beat until blended. On shallow plate, combine cheese, panko, Italian seasoning, and basil and mix well. Dip pork chops into egg mixture, then into cheese mixture, pressing the cheese mixture firmly onto the chops. Place on wire rack when coated. Let stand for 10 minutes.

2. Heat butter and olive oil in a large skillet over medium-high heat. Fry the pork chops, 2–4 minutes on each side, until brown and crisp and just slightly pink inside. Serve immediately.

Pork with Peaches

SERVES 4

¾ pound pork tenderloin
1 tablespoon soy sauce
1 tablespoon apple juice
1½ teaspoons cornstarch
1 tablespoon water
2 tablespoons plus 1 teaspoon vegetable oil, divided
1 teaspoon minced ginger, divided
2 teaspoons curry powder
2 large peaches, thinly sliced
½ cup chicken broth
Ground black pepper, to taste

1. Cut the pork into 1" cubes. Place pork in a medium bowl and toss with the soy sauce and apple juice. Let stand for 5 minutes.

2. In a small bowl, dissolve the cornstarch in the water.

3. Heat 2 tablespoons oil in a large skillet on medium-high heat. Add pork and half the ginger. Cook, stirring constantly, until pork is no longer pink and is nearly cooked through.

4. Push pork to the sides of the pan. Add 1 teaspoon oil in the middle. Add the remainder of the ginger and the curry powder. Stir for a few seconds until aromatic. Add sliced peaches. Cook for a minute, stirring continually, and then add chicken broth. Add cornstarch and water mixture, stirring to thicken.

5. Season with pepper. Cook for another minute, stirring to mix everything together. Serve hot.

Sesame Pork with Noodles

▶ SERVES 2–4

1½ teaspoons salt, divided
½ pound thin noodles, fresh or dried
½ pound lean pork, cut into thin strips about 1½" long
2 teaspoons dark soy sauce
2 teaspoons Chinese rice wine or dry sherry
1 teaspoon cornstarch
2 tablespoons vegetable or peanut oil, divided
½ teaspoon minced garlic
½ teaspoon minced ginger
1 cup shredded carrot
1 cup shredded celery
1 cup bottled toasted sesame dressing

1. In a large pot, bring 2 quarts of water to a boil with 1 teaspoon salt. Add noodles and cook until they are firm but tender. Drain the noodles.

2. Place pork in a bowl and add dark soy sauce, rice wine or dry sherry, and cornstarch. Marinate for 15 minutes.

3. Heat a wok or medium skillet over medium-high heat until it is nearly smoking. Add 1 tablespoon oil. When the oil is hot, add garlic. Stir-fry for 10 seconds, and add pork. Stir-fry pork until it is no longer pink and is nearly cooked through.

4. Push pork to the sides of the pan and heat 1 tablespoon oil in the middle. Add ginger and stir-fry for 10 seconds. Add carrot and the celery. Stir-fry for a minute, sprinkling ½ teaspoon salt over vegetables. Stir to combine vegetables with pork.

5. Stir in cooked noodles. Add sesame dressing and bring to a boil. Stir-fry for 1–2 more minutes to mix all the ingredients. Serve hot.

Spicy Hoisin Pork

▶ SERVES 4

¾ pound pork tenderloin, cut into thin slices

1 tablespoon soy sauce

2 teaspoons baking soda

1 bunch spinach

2 tablespoons hoisin sauce

1 tablespoon dark soy sauce

¼ cup water

3 tablespoons oil for stir-frying, divided

¼ teaspoon chili paste

1. Marinate pork in soy sauce and baking soda for 30 minutes.

2. Blanch spinach briefly in boiling water and drain thoroughly.

3. Combine hoisin sauce, dark soy sauce, and water. Set aside.

4. Add 2 tablespoons oil to a preheated wok or medium skillet. When oil is hot, add pork and stir-fry until it changes color and is nearly cooked through. Remove and drain on paper towels.

5. Add 1 tablespoon oil to the wok. When oil is hot, add chili paste and stir-fry until aromatic. Add blanched spinach. Stir-fry for 1 minute. Add hoisin sauce mixture in the middle of the wok and bring to a boil. Add pork. Turn down the heat and mix everything through. Serve hot.

HOW TO SEASON A CARBON STEEL WOK

It's important to properly season a wok before using it for the first time. First, wash the wok in soapy water. Dry thoroughly, then lightly coat the inside surface with vegetable oil, using a paper towel and tilting the wok to ensure even coverage. Heat the wok on low-medium heat for 10 minutes. Remove to a cool burner and wipe off the inside with a paper towel. Repeat this process several times. The wok is ready to use when the paper towel doesn't pick up any black residue.

Korean Spicy Pork Tacos

▶ SERVES 4

1 cup Korean-Inspired Marinade (see recipe in Chapter 3)
3 tablespoons gochujang paste (Korean hot pepper paste)
$\frac{1}{2}$ teaspoon red pepper flakes
$\frac{3}{4}$ pound pork loin, cut into $\frac{1}{2}$" cubes
2 tablespoons vegetable oil
$\frac{1}{4}$ cup chopped green onions
$\frac{1}{2}$ small white onion, peeled and sliced
12 corn tortillas
2 cups kimchi, chopped
1 teaspoon toasted sesame seeds
1 cup seasoned and toasted seaweed, cut into thin strips

1. In a large bowl, whisk together the marinade, gochujang paste, and red pepper flakes. Add pork and refrigerate for at least 1 hour.

2. Heat wok over medium-high heat and add the oil. Once oil is hot, stir-fry green onions and onion for 30 seconds. Add pork and stir-fry for 3–4 minutes until browned. Transfer to a plate.

3. Warm tortillas in a cast-iron skillet. Divide pork and kimchi among tortillas. Top each taco with toasted sesame seeds and seaweed strips. Serve warm.

Korean-Style Pork Stir-Fry

▶ SERVES 4

¼ cup Korean-Inspired Marinade (see recipe in Chapter 3)
2 tablespoons gochujang paste (Korean hot pepper paste)
2 tablespoons soy sauce
1 teaspoon sesame oil
½ tablespoon honey
½ tablespoon rice wine vinegar
1 pound lean pork, cut into strips
2 tablespoons vegetable oil
½ small white onion, peeled and sliced
2 cloves garlic, peeled and crushed
2 green onions, trimmed and cut into 1" pieces
1 tablespoon toasted sesame seeds

1. In a medium bowl, whisk together marinade, gochujang, soy sauce, sesame oil, honey, and vinegar. Set aside.

2. Place pork strips in a large resealable plastic bag. Pour in the marinade-gochujang mixture and add pork. Seal the bag and marinate for at least 2 hours, turning the bag occasionally so that all the pork is evenly coated.

3. Heat a wok or medium skillet over medium-high heat until it is nearly smoking and add oil. When oil is hot, stir-fry onion and garlic for 30 seconds.

4. Add pork. (Discard marinade.) Stir-fry pork for 3–4 minutes or until it is no longer pink, then add green onions. Remove from pan and garnish with toasted sesame seeds. Serve hot.

Pork Souvlaki

▶ SERVES 8

1 large onion, peeled and grated

3 cloves garlic, peeled and minced

2 teaspoons salt

$^3/_4$ teaspoon ground black pepper

$^1/_4$ cup plus 3 tablespoons vegetable oil, divided

4 teaspoons dried oregano, divided

2 pounds boneless pork butt, fat trimmed and cut into 1" cubes

2 large lemons, cut into wedges

SOAKING WOODEN SKEWERS

When using wooden skewers for grilling, always soak them in water for 2 hours before spearing the food. Soaking the skewers prevents them from burning when placed on the grill.

1. In a large bowl, whisk onion, garlic, salt, pepper, $^1/_4$ cup oil, and 2 teaspoons oregano. Add pork and toss to coat. Refrigerate pork at least 5 hours or overnight. Bring pork to room temperature before grilling.

2. Put meat onto wooden or metal skewers. Add 4 pieces of pork per skewer.

3. Preheat a gas or charcoal grill to medium-high. Brush grill surface to make sure it is thoroughly clean. When grill is ready, dip a clean tea towel in the remaining oil and wipe the grill surface with oil. Put pork on the grill and cook 3–4 minutes per side or until the pork is cooked through.

4. Sprinkle pork with the remaining 2 teaspoons oregano and serve it with lemon wedges.

Cuban Pork Chops

▶ SERVES 4

4 boneless pork loin chops
4 cloves garlic, peeled and finely chopped
2 teaspoons cumin seed
$\frac{1}{2}$ teaspoon dried oregano leaves
$\frac{1}{2}$ teaspoon salt
$\frac{1}{8}$ teaspoon cayenne pepper
2 tablespoons olive oil
$\frac{1}{4}$ cup orange juice
2 tablespoons lime juice

1. Trim excess fat from pork chops. In small bowl, combine garlic, cumin, oregano, salt, and cayenne pepper and mix well. Sprinkle this mixture on both sides of chops and rub into meat. Let stand at room temperature for 10 minutes.

2. Heat olive oil in heavy saucepan over medium heat. Add pork chops and cook for 5 minutes. Carefully turn and cook for 5 minutes on second side. Add orange juice and lime juice and bring to a simmer.

3. Cover pan and simmer chops for 5–10 minutes or until pork chops are tender and just slightly pink in the center and sauce is reduced. Serve immediately.

Orange Pork Chops

▶ SERVES 4

4 boneless pork chops, cut into 1" cubes

1 tablespoon soy sauce

1 tablespoon Chinese rice wine or Japanese sake

2 teaspoons cornstarch

3 tablespoons vegetable or peanut oil, divided

1 tablespoon minced ginger

4 medium carrots, peeled and cut on the diagonal into thin slices

1 teaspoon salt

Orange Sauce (see recipe in Chapter 3)

2 medium green onions, green parts only; finely chopped

1. Place pork cubes in a bowl and add soy sauce, rice wine or sake, and cornstarch. Marinate in the refrigerator for 30 minutes.

2. Heat a wok or medium skillet on medium-high heat. Add 2 tablespoons oil. When oil is hot, add pork. Let it brown for a minute, then stir-fry, stirring and moving the pork around the pan until it is no longer pink and is nearly cooked through. Remove pork and drain in a colander or on paper towels.

3. Heat 1 tablespoon oil in the wok or skillet. When oil is hot, add ginger. Stir-fry for 10 seconds, then add carrots. Stir-fry for 2 minutes, stirring in salt.

4. Add Orange Sauce and bring to a boil. Add pork back into the pan. Stir in chopped green onions. Stir-fry until everything is mixed together and pork is cooked through. Serve hot.

Southwest Pork Chops

▶ SERVES 6

3 tablespoons olive oil
6 ($\frac{1}{2}$") boneless pork chops
1 teaspoon salt
$\frac{1}{8}$ teaspoon cayenne pepper
1 tablespoon chili powder

1 chipotle chile in adobo sauce, minced
2 tablespoons adobo sauce
$\frac{1}{2}$ cup salsa
1 (8-ounce) can tomato sauce

1. Heat olive oil in heavy skillet over medium heat. Meanwhile, sprinkle pork chops with salt, cayenne pepper, and chili powder and rub into meat. Add pork chops to skillet and cook for 4 minutes.

2. Meanwhile, combine chipotle chili, adobo sauce, salsa, and tomato sauce in a small bowl. Turn pork chops and cook for 2 minutes. Then add tomato sauce mixture to skillet, bring to a simmer, and simmer for 4–6 minutes, until chops are cooked and tender.

Grilled Polish Sausages

▶ SERVES 6

6 Polish sausages
1 cup beer
3 cups coleslaw mix

$\frac{3}{4}$ cup coleslaw dressing
6 whole-wheat hot dog buns, split

1. Prepare and preheat grill. Prick sausages with fork and place in saucepan with beer. Bring to a boil over high heat, then reduce heat to low and simmer for 5 minutes, turning frequently. Drain sausages and place on grill over medium coals; grill until hot and crisp, turning occasionally, about 5–7 minutes.

2. Meanwhile, combine coleslaw mix and dressing in medium bowl and toss. Toast hot dog buns, cut-side down, on grill. Make sandwiches using sausages, coleslaw mix, and buns.

Sausage Stir-Fry

▶ SERVES 4

1 pound sweet Italian sausages
¼ cup water
2 tablespoons olive oil
1 onion, chopped
2 medium yellow summer squash, sliced
1 cup frozen broccoli florets, thawed
¾ cup sweet-and-sour sauce

SAUSAGES

Almost any sausage can be substituted for another. Just be sure to read the package to see if the sausages you choose are fully cooked or raw. The fully cooked sausages need only to be reheated, but the raw ones should be cooked until a meat thermometer registers 170°F.

1. In large skillet, cook Italian sausage and water over medium heat for 6–8 minutes, turning frequently during cooking time, until water evaporates and sausages begin to brown. Remove sausages to plate and cut into 1" pieces.

2. Drain fat from skillet but do not rinse. Return to medium-high heat, add olive oil, then add onion. Stir-fry until onion is crisp-tender, 3–4 minutes. Add squash and broccoli; stir-fry for 4–5 minutes longer, until broccoli is hot and squash is tender. Return sausage pieces to skillet along with sweet-and-sour sauce. Stir-fry for 4–6 minutes, until sausage pieces are thoroughly cooked and sauce bubbles. Serve immediately.

Sausage Quesadillas

▶ SERVES 4

1 pound bulk pork sausage
1 onion, peeled and chopped
1 red bell pepper, sliced
$\frac{1}{2}$ teaspoon paprika
$\frac{1}{2}$ teaspoon ground cumin
2 teaspoons chili powder
8 (10") flour tortillas
2 cups shredded Co-Jack cheese
2 tablespoons olive oil

TORTILLAS

Tortillas are available in two types, corn and flour. Flour tortillas are usually larger, used for quesadillas and burritos. They can be flavored with spinach, red pepper, garlic, and tomato. Flavored corn tortillas are also available, as well as the traditional white, yellow, and blue corn varieties.

1. Preheat oven to 375°F. In heavy skillet, cook pork sausage with onion over medium heat, stirring to break up sausage, about 4–5 minutes. When browned, drain off most of the fat. Add red bell pepper; cook and stir for 2–3 minutes. Sprinkle with paprika, cumin, and chili powder and remove from heat.

2. Lay 4 tortillas on work surface. Sprinkle each with ¼ cup cheese and top with one-fourth of the sausage mixture. Sprinkle with remaining cheese and top with remaining tortillas. Place on two cookie sheets and brush quesadillas with olive oil. Bake for 7–10 minutes, or until cheese is melted and tortillas are lightly browned. Cut into wedges and serve.

One-Dish Sausage and Rice

SERVES 2

1 cup chicken broth

1 cup long-grain instant rice

2 tablespoons olive oil

1 shallot, peeled and chopped

1 teaspoon paprika

8 ounces cooked smoked sausage, thinly sliced

2 sprigs fresh parsley, chopped

Salt and pepper, to taste

1. Bring chicken broth to a boil in a medium saucepan. Stir in rice, making sure all grains are moistened. Remove from heat, cover, and let stand for 5 minutes.

2. While rice is cooking, prepare other ingredients: Heat olive oil in a large skillet over medium-high heat. Add shallot. Sauté until softened, about 4 minutes (turn the heat down if the shallot is cooking too quickly). Stir in paprika.

3. Stir in sausage and parsley. Cook for a minute until sausage is heated.

4. After rice has been standing for 5 minutes, uncover and use a fork to fluff.

5. Stir sausage and parsley into cooked rice. Season with salt and pepper if desired. Serve immediately.

POULTRY MAIN DISHES

Greek Chicken Stir-Fry

▶ SERVES 4

1 pound boneless, skinless chicken
    breasts
Salt and ground black pepper to taste
2 tablespoons olive oil
2 cloves garlic, peeled and minced
2 cups frozen bell pepper and
    onion stir-fry
2 tablespoons lemon juice
$\frac{1}{2}$ cup crumbled feta cheese

> **GREEK FOOD**
>
> Seasonings and ingredients that add a Greek flavor include feta cheese, oregano, olives, spinach, phyllo dough, pita bread, rice, fresh seafood, grape leaves, lamb, and yogurt. The food is fairly spicy, with some unusual food combinations that include spinach and raisins, and beef and olives.

1. Cut chicken breasts into 1" pieces and sprinkle with salt and pepper. Heat olive oil in a wok or large skillet over medium-high heat. Add chicken and garlic and stir-fry until chicken is cooked, about 4 minutes. Remove chicken and garlic to plate with slotted spoon and set aside.

2. Add frozen vegetables to skillet and stir-fry for 5–7 minutes until hot and crisp-tender. Add chicken to skillet and sprinkle with lemon juice. Stir-fry for 1 minute longer. Sprinkle with feta cheese, remove pan from heat, cover, and let stand for 2–3 minutes longer to melt cheese. Serve immediately.

Parmesan Chicken

 SERVES 6

6 boneless, skinless chicken breasts
$\frac{1}{4}$ cup lemon juice
1 teaspoon salt
$\frac{1}{8}$ teaspoon pepper
$\frac{1}{2}$ teaspoon dried thyme
$\frac{1}{4}$ cup unsalted butter
$\frac{1}{2}$ cup grated Parmesan cheese

1. Cut chicken breasts into 1" pieces. Sprinkle with lemon juice, salt, pepper, and thyme leaves. Let stand at room temperature for 10 minutes.

2. Melt butter in a heavy saucepan over medium heat. Sauté chicken until thoroughly cooked, about 5–6 minutes, stirring frequently. Sprinkle cheese over chicken, turn off heat, cover pan, and let stand for 2–3 minutes to melt cheese. Serve over hot cooked couscous.

Creamy Chicken over Rice

▶ SERVES 4-6

1½ cups Jasmati rice

2½ cups water

4 boneless, skinless chicken breasts

1 teaspoon salt

⅛ teaspoon ground black pepper

3 tablespoons olive oil

1 onion, peeled and finely chopped

1 (10-ounce) container refrigerated four-cheese Alfredo sauce

1 (3-ounce) package cream cheese, softened

AROMATIC RICE VARIETIES

There are lots of different rice varieties available in the supermarket. Jasmati rice is the American version of jasmine rice, a fragrant long-grain rice that cooks quickly and is always fluffy. You can find basmati, Texmati, Wehani, Louisiana pecan, Della, and jasmine. These rices smell like nuts or popcorn while they cook.

1. In heavy saucepan, combine rice and water; bring to a boil over high heat. Cover, reduce heat to low, and simmer for 15–20 minutes, until rice is tender. Meanwhile, cut chicken into 1" pieces and sprinkle with salt and pepper. Heat olive oil in a large saucepan over medium heat. Add onion; cook and stir until crisp-tender, about 3–4 minutes. Add chicken; cook and stir until chicken is thoroughly cooked, about 5–6 minutes.

2. Add Alfredo sauce and cream cheese to chicken mixture; cook and stir over low heat until sauce bubbles. When rice is tender, fluff with fork. Serve chicken over rice.

Herb-Crusted Chicken Breasts

▶ SERVES 6

1 cup buttermilk
1 teaspoon salt
$\frac{1}{8}$ teaspoon cayenne pepper
6 boneless, skinless chicken breasts
3 slices bread
$\frac{1}{2}$ teaspoon dried thyme leaves
$\frac{1}{2}$ teaspoon dried basil leaves
$\frac{1}{2}$ teaspoon dried tarragon
$\frac{1}{2}$ cup grated Parmesan cheese
$\frac{1}{3}$ cup olive oil

1. Heat oven to 375°F. In large bowl, combine buttermilk with salt and cayenne pepper and mix well. Add chicken breasts, turn to coat, and set aside.

2. Place bread on cookie sheet and bake at 375°F until crisp, about 5–7 minutes. Remove from oven and break into pieces. Place in blender or food processor; blend or process until crumbs are fine. Pour crumbs onto large plate and add herbs and cheese; mix well.

3. Remove chicken from buttermilk mixture and roll in crumb mixture to coat. Set on wire rack. In a heavy skillet, heat olive oil over medium heat. Add chicken, 2 pieces at a time, and cook for 2–3 minutes on each side until browned. Remove to cookie sheet. Repeat to brown remaining chicken. Bake chicken at 375°F for 12–14 minutes or until thoroughly cooked. Serve immediately.

Green Chili Chicken Burritos

▶ SERVES 6

2 (9-ounce) packages grilled chicken
   strips
1 (4-ounce) can chopped green chilies,
   drained
1 cup sour cream
$\frac{1}{4}$ teaspoon cayenne pepper
6 flour tortillas
$1\frac{1}{2}$ cups shredded pepper jack cheese,
   divided

SPICE IT UP

There are lots of ingredients you can use to add spice to your food. Canned chopped green chilies, jalapeño peppers, salsas, taco sauce, and chili powder are all good choices. You can also use cayenne pepper, Tabasco sauce, fresh chilies like habaneros and Anaheim peppers, and ground dried chilies.

1. Preheat oven to 400°F. In microwave-safe bowl, combine chicken strips and green chilies. Microwave on medium power for 2–3 minutes, stirring once during cooking time, until ingredients are hot. Stir in sour cream and cayenne pepper.

2. Divide mixture among tortillas. Sprinkle with 1 cup of cheese. Roll up to enclose filling. Place in 2-quart casserole dish and top with remaining cheese. Bake for 7–11 minutes, until cheese melts and burritos are hot.

Microwave Salsa Chicken

▶ SERVES 4

1½ cups chicken broth
2 tablespoons chili powder
½ teaspoon salt
⅛ teaspoon cayenne pepper
4 boneless, skinless chicken breasts
1 cup chunky salsa
2 tablespoons tomato paste
2 tomatoes, chopped

TOMATO PASTE

Tomato paste is a concentrate of fresh tomatoes, sometimes made with seasonings like basil, garlic, and oregano. You can find it in cans or in tubes. Purchase it in tubes and you can add a small amount to dishes without having to store leftover paste.

1. Place chicken broth into a microwave-safe dish. Microwave on high for 3–5 minutes, until boiling. Meanwhile, sprinkle chili powder, salt, and cayenne pepper on the chicken and rub into both sides. Pierce chicken on the smooth side with a fork. Carefully place, smooth-side down, in hot liquid in dish.

2. Microwave chicken on high power for 8 minutes, then carefully drain off chicken broth. Meanwhile, in small bowl, combine salsa, tomato paste, and tomatoes and mix well. Turn chicken over, rearrange chicken in dish, and pour salsa mixture over. Return to microwave and cook for 2–6 minutes, checking every 2 minutes, until chicken is thoroughly cooked. Let stand for 5 minutes and serve.

Microwave Chicken Divan

▶ SERVES 4

1½ cups chicken broth
½ teaspoon salt
⅛ teaspoon ground black pepper
½ teaspoon dried thyme leaves
4 boneless, skinless chicken breasts
1 (10-ounce) package frozen broccoli, thawed
1 (10-ounce) container refrigerated four-cheese Alfredo sauce
1 cup crushed round buttery crackers

1. Place chicken broth into a microwave-safe dish. Microwave on high for 3–5 minutes, until boiling. Meanwhile, sprinkle salt, pepper, and thyme on the chicken and rub into both sides. Pierce chicken on the smooth side with a fork. Carefully place, smooth-side down, in hot liquid in dish.

2. Microwave chicken on high power for 8 minutes, then carefully drain off chicken broth. Meanwhile, drain thawed broccoli and combine in medium bowl with Alfredo sauce. Rearrange chicken in dish, turn over, and pour broccoli mixture over; sprinkle with cracker crumbs. Return to microwave and cook for 3–6 minutes, checking every 2 minutes, until chicken is thoroughly cooked. Let stand for 5 minutes and serve.

Quick Chicken Cordon Bleu

▶ SERVES 4

1 cup grated Parmesan cheese, divided

4 boneless, skinless chicken breasts

8 slices pancetta

1 (14-ounce) jar Alfredo sauce

4 slices Baby Swiss cheese

DECONSTRUCTING RECIPES

One way to make recipes simpler to make is to deconstruct them. Chicken cordon bleu is typically made by stuffing ham and cheese into chicken breasts and then baking them. Wrapping the chicken in pancetta and topping with cheese results in the same taste but is much quicker to make.

1. Preheat oven to 400°F. Place ½ cup Parmesan cheese on a plate and dip chicken breasts into cheese to coat. Wrap 2 slices of pancetta around each chicken breast and place in a 2-quart casserole dish. Bake for 10 minutes.

2. In medium bowl, combine Alfredo sauce with remaining ½ cup Parmesan cheese.

3. Remove casserole from oven and pour Alfredo sauce mixture over chicken. Return to oven and bake for 10 minutes longer. Top each chicken breast with a slice of cheese and return to the oven. Bake for 5 minutes longer, or until chicken is thoroughly cooked and cheese is melted. Serve immediately.

Stir-Fry Chicken Cacciatore

▶ SERVES 4

1 pound boneless, skinless chicken thighs

$3\frac{1}{2}$ tablespoons dry white wine, divided

1 teaspoon dried oregano

Ground black pepper, to taste

2 teaspoons cornstarch

3 tablespoons low-sodium chicken broth

3 tablespoons diced tomatoes with juice

$\frac{1}{2}$ teaspoon sugar

3 tablespoons olive oil, divided

1 shallot, peeled and chopped

$\frac{1}{4}$ pound sliced fresh mushrooms

1 red bell pepper, seeded, cut into thin strips

1 tablespoon chopped fresh oregano

1. Cut chicken into thin strips about 2"–3" long. Place chicken strips in a bowl and add $2\frac{1}{2}$ tablespoons white wine, oregano, pepper, and cornstarch, adding cornstarch last. Let chicken stand. In bowl, combine chicken broth, diced tomatoes, and sugar. Set aside.

2. Heat 1 tablespoon oil in a wok or heavy skillet. When oil is hot, add chopped shallot. Stir-fry for a minute, until it begins to soften, and then add sliced mushrooms. Stir-fry for a minute; then add red bell pepper. Stir-fry for another minute, adding a bit of water if vegetables begin to dry out. Remove vegetables from the pan.

3. Heat 2 tablespoons oil in the wok or skillet. When oil is hot, add chicken. Let chicken brown for a minute; then stir-fry for about 5 minutes, until it turns white and is nearly cooked through. Splash 1 tablespoon of white wine on chicken while stir-frying.

4. Add chicken broth and tomato mixture to the middle of the pan. Bring to a boil. Return vegetables to the pan. Stir in fresh oregano. Cook, stirring, for another couple of minutes to mix everything together. Serve immediately.

Pan-Fried Garlic Chicken Thighs with Sun-Dried Tomatoes

▶ SERVES 2

1 pound (6–8 small) boneless, skinless chicken thighs

$\frac{1}{8}$ teaspoon garlic salt

$\frac{1}{4}$ teaspoon ground black pepper

2 teaspoons olive oil

$\frac{1}{2}$ medium onion, peeled and thinly sliced

2 tablespoons sun-dried tomato strips

$\frac{1}{2}$ cup chicken broth

2 teaspoons lemon juice

1 tablespoon chopped fresh basil leaves

COOKING WITH OLIVE OIL

Loaded with heart-healthy monounsaturated fats, olive oil is a great choice for pan-frying, sautéing, and stir-frying. Just be sure to stick with the olive oils that don't break down at high heats (such as pure olive oil) and leave the extra-virgin olive oil for salads. Always wait until the olive oil is fully heated before adding the food.

1. Rinse chicken thighs and pat dry. Rub garlic salt and pepper over the chicken to season.

2. Heat olive oil in a large skillet over medium heat. Add chicken. Cook for 5–6 minutes, until browned on both sides, turning over halfway through cooking. Stir chicken occasionally to make sure it doesn't stick to the pan.

3. Push chicken to the sides of the pan. Add onion and sun-dried tomato strips. Cook in oil for about 3 minutes, until onion is browned.

4. Add chicken broth. Stir in lemon juice.

5. Simmer for 8–10 minutes, until liquid is nearly absorbed and chicken is just cooked through. Stir in basil leaves during the last 2 minutes of cooking. Serve immediately.

Quick and Easy Curry Chicken

▶ SERVES 2

4 tablespoons oil, or as needed

1 heaping teaspoon minced ginger

1 clove garlic, peeled and minced

1 tablespoon mild curry powder

2 boneless, skinless chicken breasts, cut into 1" cubes

1 (8-ounce) can bamboo shoots, drained

1 (8-ounce) can water chestnuts, drained

2 teaspoons soy sauce

¼ cup chicken broth

2 medium green onions, trimmed and sliced into thin strips

1. Add 2 tablespoons oil to a preheated wok or medium skillet. When oil is hot, add ginger, garlic, and curry powder. Stir-fry until there is a strong odor of curry. Add chicken and stir-fry for about 5 minutes until chicken is well mixed with the curry powder. Remove and set aside.

2. Add bamboo shoots, water chestnuts, and soy sauce to the wok. Cook for 1–2 minutes, or until bamboo shoots and water chestnuts are heated through and coated in curry.

3. Add chicken back into the wok. Add chicken broth. Bring to a boil, cover, and simmer until everything is cooked through. Stir in green onions or add as a garnish.

CURRY—MORE THAN A POWDER

Although we tend to think of curry as a spice or blend of spices, the word has its origins in the Tamil word *karhi*, a spicy sauce. We have a British official to thank for the association of curry with a dry powder. The story is that, when leaving India, the official ordered his servant to prepare a compilation of spices so that he could enjoy his favorite Indian dishes upon returning home to Britain. Freshly made curry powder is preferable to commercially prepared brands. Still, in today's busy world it's not always possible to find time for chopping herbs and grinding fresh spices. Although this recipe uses a mild curry powder, the hotter Madras curry powders generally work best in Chinese dishes.

Chicken Lo Mein

▶ SERVES 4

8 ounces fresh egg noodles
$\frac{1}{2}$ cup mushrooms, fresh or dried
2 tablespoons oyster sauce
1 tablespoon soy sauce
1 teaspoon sugar
1 teaspoon Chinese rice wine or dry sherry
$\frac{1}{2}$ cup water
3 tablespoons vegetable oil, divided
4 cabbage leaves, shredded
$\frac{1}{4}$ teaspoon salt
$\frac{1}{2}$ cup mung bean sprouts, rinsed and drained
1 cup boneless, skinless cooked chicken, thinly sliced

1. In a large pot of water, boil noodles until the flour is removed and they are tender, about 5 minutes. Drain thoroughly.

2. If using dried mushrooms, soak them in hot water for at least 20 minutes to soften. Slice mushrooms.

3. In a small bowl, combine oyster sauce, soy sauce, sugar, rice wine, and water, and set aside.

4. Add 2 tablespoons of oil to a preheated wok or medium skillet. When oil is hot, add cabbage leaves. Stir-fry until they turn bright green and are tender. Season with salt. Add 1 tablespoon of oil.

5. Add mushrooms. Stir-fry briefly, then add bean sprouts.

6. Add prepared sauce in the middle of the wok. Bring to a boil. Turn down heat slightly and add chicken. Add noodles. Mix everything through and serve hot.

Soy Sauce Chicken

▶ SERVES 2

1 teaspoon Chinese five-spice powder

1 tablespoon cornstarch

2 chicken legs

$\frac{1}{2}$ cup soy sauce

$\frac{3}{4}$ cup water

2 tablespoons Chinese rice wine or
    dry sherry

4 teaspoons brown sugar

3–4 cups oil for deep-frying

1 large clove garlic, peeled and minced

1 slice ginger, minced

FROM MARINADE TO SAUCE

When a marinade does double duty as a sauce it's important to ensure that it is thoroughly cooked. As an added precaution, you can bring the marinade to boil in a saucepan before adding it to the wok.

1. In a large bowl, mix five-spice powder and cornstarch. Mix in with chicken and marinate for 30 minutes.

2. In a medium bowl, mix soy sauce, water, rice wine, and brown sugar. Set aside.

3. Heat oil in a wok. When oil reaches 325°F, deep-fry chicken legs until browned. Remove with a slotted spoon and drain on paper towels.

4. Drain all but 2 tablespoons oil out of the wok. Add garlic and ginger and stir-fry briefly until aromatic. Add the sauce. Add chicken, cover, and simmer for 15–20 minutes until chicken is thoroughly cooked.

Poultry Main Dishes

Kung Pao Chicken

▶ SERVES 4

1 pound boneless, skinless chicken thighs, cut into 1" cubes
1½ teaspoons plus 1 tablespoon cornstarch, divided
2 teaspoons light soy sauce
½ teaspoon salt
1 teaspoon sugar
1 teaspoon rice wine vinegar
1 cup water
2½ teaspoons peanut oil, divided
1 teaspoon chili paste with garlic
2 thin slices fresh ginger
2 cloves garlic, peeled and thinly sliced
1 teaspoon Shaoxing rice wine or medium-dry sherry
3 tablespoons garlic chives or other chives, cut into 2" segments

1. Mix chicken with 1½ teaspoons of cornstarch, soy sauce, and salt in a medium bowl. Stir well and set aside.

2. In a small bowl, mix sugar, vinegar, remaining cornstarch, and water. Set aside.

3. Heat a wok over high heat. Add 1 teaspoon of oil and swirl to coat the pan. When the oil is thoroughly heated, add chicken and stir-fry until seared, about 2 minutes. Transfer chicken to paper towels to drain.

4. Wipe the wok clean. Return to medium-high heat. Add remaining 1½ teaspoons of oil, chili paste, ginger, and garlic. Stir-fry for 30 seconds. Add chicken, wine, vinegar-cornstarch mixture, and chives. Stir-fry until chicken is thoroughly cooked, about 2 more minutes. Serve hot.

Szechuan-Style Chicken Wings

▶ SERVES 3

2 pounds chicken wings, tips clipped
3 teaspoons red pepper flakes
1 tablespoon orange zest
$\frac{1}{2}$ cup freshly squeezed orange juice
$\frac{1}{2}$ tablespoon fresh ginger, peeled and minced
2 teaspoons garlic, peeled and minced
1 tablespoon honey
3 tablespoons sesame oil
$\frac{1}{4}$ cup soy sauce
$\frac{1}{4}$ cup chopped green onions
$\frac{1}{4}$ teaspoon garlic salt
$\frac{1}{4}$ cup vegetable oil
2 teaspoons cornstarch
1 tablespoon water

1. Rinse chicken under cold, running water and pat dry with paper towels. Combine pepper flakes, orange zest, juice, ginger, garlic, honey, sesame oil, soy sauce, green onions, and garlic salt in a medium-sized bowl and mix to combine. Add chicken wings and stir to coat. Refrigerate until ready to use. (The recipe can be made ahead of time up this point and kept refrigerated as long as overnight.)

2. Heat vegetable oil in a large nonstick skillet over medium-high heat. Use a slotted spoon to transfer wings from marinade to pan. Reserve marinade.

3. Cook wings until browned on both sides, about 5–6 minutes per side.

4. Mix cornstarch with water, stirring until smooth. Add reserved marinade to chicken wings and bring to a simmer over medium heat. Slowly stir in cornstarch mixture and stir until blended. Simmer for 5–6 minutes until thick and bubbly. Taste and adjust seasoning as desired. Serve hot.

Asian Sesame Chicken Skewers

▶ SERVES 8

24–30 (6") wooden skewers
$\frac{1}{2}$ cup canned low-sodium chicken stock
$\frac{1}{4}$ cup chopped fresh cilantro, plus extra for garnish
2 tablespoons tamari or low-sodium soy sauce
2 tablespoons sesame oil
2 cloves garlic, peeled and minced
4–5 drops (or to taste) hot sauce
$1\frac{1}{2}$ pounds boneless, skinless chicken breasts (about 6 halves)
2 tablespoons (approximately) black sesame seeds, for garnish

1. Place wooden skewers in a tall glass of water to soak for at least 15 minutes while preparing chicken. (This will help prevent them from burning under the broiler.)

2. To make marinade, combine stock, cilantro, tamari, sesame oil, garlic, and hot sauce in a medium-sized bowl; whisk until blended.

3. Rinse chicken under cold, running water and pat dry with paper towels. Cut chicken into $\frac{1}{2}$"-wide strips the length of the breast. You should have about 18–24 strips. (The strips will vary somewhat in size.) Add chicken strips to marinade, cover, and refrigerate for 15 minutes.

4. Just before preparing to serve, lightly oil a broiler rack and position it about 4" from the heat source. Preheat oven broiler to medium.

5. Remove chicken strips from marinade and discard marinade. Thread 1 strip on a presoaked wooden skewer. Thread remaining chicken on remaining skewers. (Threading chicken in the form of an S will help them stay on the skewer.)

6. Place skewers on the broiler rack and broil for about 3 minutes. Turn skewers over and broil for another 3–4 minutes, until chicken is no longer pink. Remove from oven and sprinkle with sesame seeds and chopped cilantro. Serve hot.

Chicken Souvlaki

2 pounds boneless, skinless chicken thighs, cut into 1" cubes
⅓ cup extra-virgin olive oil
2 medium onions, peeled and grated
4 cloves garlic, peeled and minced
2 tablespoons grated lemon zest
1 teaspoon dried oregano
1 teaspoon chopped fresh rosemary leaves
2 teaspoons salt
1 teaspoon ground black pepper
2 tablespoons fresh lemon juice

1. In a large bowl, combine chicken, oil, onions, garlic, lemon zest, oregano, rosemary, salt, and pepper. Toss to coat. Cover bowl with plastic wrap and refrigerate 8 hours or overnight. Take chicken out of the refrigerator 30 minutes before skewering.

2. Preheat a gas or charcoal grill to medium-high. Put chicken onto wooden or metal skewers; each skewer should hold 4 pieces.

3. Place skewers on grill and grill 3–4 minutes per side or until chicken is no longer pink inside.

4. Drizzle lemon juice over skewers and serve.

Ginger-Orange Chicken Breast

▶ SERVES 1

1 (5-ounce) boneless, skinless chicken breast
1 tablespoon butter
$\frac{1}{8}$ teaspoon seasoned salt
Freshly ground black pepper, to taste
1 clove garlic, peeled and minced
2 teaspoons grated fresh ginger
1 teaspoon orange zest
2 tablespoons orange juice

1. Rinse chicken under cold, running water and pat dry with paper towels. Melt butter in a small nonstick skillet over medium-high heat. Season the chicken with salt and pepper. Brown chicken, turning once, about 8 minutes per side. Transfer chicken to a plate and keep warm.

2. Add garlic to the pan and cook for about 1 minute, stirring frequently to prevent burning. Add ginger, orange zest, and juice, and bring to a simmer. Add chicken and any reserved juices and heat through, about 4–5 minutes. Cut through bottom of chicken to make sure it is cooked. Adjust seasoning to taste. Serve hot with the sauce.

Chianti Chicken

▶ SERVES 4

3 cloves garlic, peeled and minced

2 tablespoons finely chopped lemon verbena or lemon thyme

2 tablespoons finely chopped fresh parsley

2¼ teaspoons salt, divided

5 tablespoons extra-virgin olive oil, divided

4 bone-in chicken quarters (legs and thighs)

¾ teaspoon ground black pepper

2 tablespoons unsalted butter, divided

2 cups red grapes (in clusters)

1 medium red onion, peeled and sliced

1 cup Chianti red wine

1 cup chicken or vegetable stock

CHIANTI

Chianti is a wine-growing region in Tuscany (near Florence, Italy). Its gentle rolling hills contain a mix of olive groves and vineyards.

1. Preheat oven to 400°F.

2. In a small bowl, whisk garlic, lemon verbena, parsley, ¼ teaspoon salt, and 2 tablespoons oil.

3. Season chicken with remaining salt and pepper. Place your finger under the skin of a chicken thigh and loosen it by moving your finger back and forth to create a pocket. Spread ¼ of garlic-herb mixture into pocket. Repeat the process with remaining chicken quarters.

4. Heat remaining oil and 1 tablespoon butter in a large oven-safe pot over medium-high heat 30 seconds. Add chicken quarters and brown 3–4 minutes per side.

5. Top chicken with grapes. Transfer pot to oven and roast the chicken 20–30 minutes or until internal temperature reaches 180°F. Remove chicken and grapes from the pot and keep them warm. Remove excess fat from the pot.

Poultry Main Dishes

Chianti Chicken—continued

6. Return pot to the stovetop over medium heat, add onions, and cook 3–4 minutes. Add wine and stock and increase heat to medium-high. Bring mixture to a boil, then reduce heat to medium-low. Cook sauce until it thickens, about 30 minutes. Remove from heat and stir in remaining butter.

7. To serve, put some of the sauce on a plate and top with chicken and grapes. Serve with extra sauce on the side.

Five-Ingredient Greek Chicken

▶ SERVES 6

6 (5-ounce) bone-in chicken thighs, skinned
$\frac{1}{2}$ cup Kalamata olives
1 (6.5-ounce) jar artichoke hearts in olive oil, undrained
1 pint cherry tomatoes
$\frac{1}{4}$ cup chopped parsley

1. Place chicken, olives, artichokes and artichoke oil, and cherry tomatoes in a 4- to 5-quart slow cooker.

2. Cover and cook on low 4–6 hours. Serve in large bowls garnished with parsley.

Chicken Paprika

1 (5-ounce) boneless, skinless chicken breast
Pinch garlic salt
Freshly ground black pepper, to taste
1 tablespoon olive oil
1 clove garlic, peeled and minced
1 teaspoon Hungarian paprika
$\frac{1}{3}$ cup chicken stock
$\frac{1}{4}$ cup sour cream, at room temperature
2 tablespoons chopped fresh parsley

1. Rinse chicken under cold, running water and pat dry with paper towels. Season with garlic salt and pepper. Heat oil in a small nonstick skillet over medium-high heat. Cook chicken until lightly browned, about 4–5 minutes per side. Transfer chicken to a plate and cover with tinfoil to keep warm.

2. Reduce heat to medium-low and add garlic, paprika, and chicken stock, stirring to combine. Bring to a simmer and cook until slightly reduced, about 5 minutes. Reduce heat to low and add sour cream, whisking constantly to blend.

3. Return chicken and any accumulated juices to the pan and cook until chicken is cooked through, about 5 minutes. Serve with sauce ladled over chicken and garnished with parsley.

Chicken Apple Sausages with Dijon Glaze

▶ SERVES 1

6 ounces gourmet chicken and apple sausage

1 tablespoon Dijon mustard

1 teaspoon Worcestershire sauce

1 teaspoon minced garlic

1 tablespoon ketchup

1 tablespoon olive oil

Pinch garlic salt

Freshly ground black pepper, to taste

1. Cut sausages into 1½" pieces. Combine Dijon, Worcestershire, garlic, and ketchup in a small bowl and mix until blended.

2. Heat oil in a small nonstick skillet over medium heat and add sausage pieces; cook, stirring frequently, until just starting to brown, about 5–6 minutes. Add Dijon glaze and stir to coat sausages. Season with garlic salt and pepper. Cook until heated through, about 2 minutes. Serve hot with the pan glaze.

Sicilian Chicken

▷ SERVES 4

4 boneless, skinless chicken breast halves
$1/4$ teaspoon salt
Freshly ground black pepper, to taste
2 tablespoons olive oil, divided
1 cup thinly sliced red onion
$1/2$ cup bell pepper strips, assorted colors (about $1/4$" strips)
2 cloves garlic, peeled and minced
$1/3$ cup chopped fresh basil, divided
2 tablespoons quality balsamic vinegar
$1/4$–$1/2$ teaspoon (to taste) red pepper flakes

1. Rinse chicken under cold, running water and pat dry with paper towels. Season with salt and pepper.

2. Heat 2 tablespoons of oil in a medium-sized nonstick skillet over medium-high heat. Cook chicken until golden brown, about 4–5 minutes per side. Transfer chicken to a plate and tent with tinfoil to keep warm.

3. Add onions and peppers to the skillet; sauté until soft, about 4 minutes, stirring frequently. Add garlic and sauté for about 1 minute, stirring frequently. Add half of the basil, the vinegar, and red pepper flakes; stir to combine.

4. Add chicken and any accumulated juices. Cover and reduce heat to medium. Simmer until chicken is cooked through, about 4–6 minutes. Taste and adjust seasoning as desired. Serve hot, garnished with remaining basil.

Soft Tacos with Spicy Chicken Breasts

▶ SERVES 2

2 (6-ounce) boneless, skinless chicken breast halves
Garlic salt, to taste
Cayenne pepper, to taste
1 tablespoon vegetable oil
3/4 cup salsa, divided
1 tablespoon chopped fresh cilantro, plus extra for garnish
2 (8") low-carb tortillas
1/4 cup shredded pepper jack cheese
1/4 cup seeded and diced tomato
1/2 cup shredded romaine lettuce leaves
1/3 cup diced avocado
1/4 cup sour cream

1. Rinse chicken under cold, running water and pat dry with paper towels. Cut chicken across the grain into 1/2" strips. Season with garlic salt and cayenne.

2. Heat oil in a medium-sized nonstick skillet over medium-high heat. Cook chicken until almost done, about 5 minutes, stirring frequently. Add 1/4 cup of salsa and stir to combine. Bring to a simmer and finish cooking chicken, about 2–3 minutes. Remove from heat and stir in 1 tablespoon of cilantro.

3. To serve, place each tortilla on a serving plate. Equally divide chicken between the tortillas. Top with equal amounts of cheese, tomato, lettuce, and avocado. Serve remaining salsa and sour cream on the side. Garnish with cilantro leaves.

Chicken Cutlets with Grainy Mustard

▶ SERVES 4

4 boneless, skinless chicken breast halves, cut in thirds and lightly pounded

1/3 teaspoon salt

Freshly ground black pepper, to taste

3 tablespoons butter

3 tablespoons grainy mustard

1/3 cup dry white wine

1/2 cup chicken stock

1/4 cup heavy cream, at room temperature

2 tablespoons chopped fresh parsley

1. Rinse chicken under cold, running water and pat dry with paper towels. Season with salt and pepper.

2. Melt butter in a large nonstick skillet over medium-high heat. Add chicken pieces in a single layer; sauté until golden, turning once, about 6 minutes total. Transfer chicken to a plate and set aside.

3. Add mustard, wine, and stock to pan and bring to a simmer, stirring and scraping up any browned bits from the bottom of pan.

4. Simmer about 4 minutes, until slightly reduced.

POUNDING CHICKEN BREASTS

Lightly pounding chicken breasts reduces the cooking time. To prepare, start with boneless, skinless breast halves that have been rinsed under cold, running water and patted dry with paper towels. Cut each breast into 3 even-sized pieces and line a workspace with plastic wrap. Lay the chicken pieces in a single layer and top with another layer of plastic wrap. Use the flat side of a meat mallet or the bottom of a small, heavy skillet to lightly and evenly pound the pieces several times to flatten, starting from the center of each piece and working your way out to the ends. The pieces should end up about 1/2" thick. Transfer pieces to a tray and repeat with remaining chicken. When complete, sanitize the entire work surface, even though it was covered with plastic wrap.

Chicken Cutlets with Grainy Mustard—continued

5. Reduce heat to medium-low and slowly add cream, stirring constantly to incorporate. Simmer for about 2 minutes.

6. Add chicken and any accumulated juices, and cook until chicken is heated through, about 2 minutes. Taste and adjust seasoning as desired. Serve hot, garnished with chopped parsley.

Chicken with Pepper Cream Sauce

▶ SERVES 4

3 tablespoons olive oil
4 (5-ounce) boneless, skinless chicken breasts
$\frac{1}{2}$ teaspoon kosher salt
1 tablespoon butter
$\frac{1}{4}$ cup diced roasted red peppers
1 cup grated Parmesan cheese
2 cups heavy cream, at room temperature
3–4 tablespoons (to taste) hot pepper sauce
2 tablespoons chopped fresh parsley

1. Heat oil in medium-sized nonstick skillet over medium-high heat. Season the chicken with salt, then sear chicken until cooked through, about 7 minutes per side. Transfer chicken to a plate and tent with tinfoil to keep warm.

2. Melt butter over medium-low heat in the same skillet. Add red peppers, Parmesan, cream, and hot pepper sauce. Bring to a simmer, whisking frequently. Cook until slightly reduced, about 10 minutes.

3. To serve, transfer chicken breasts and any accumulated juices to individual serving plates. Top chicken with sauce. Garnish with parsley, and serve hot.

Buffalo Wings

2 pounds chicken wings (about 10–12 wings)
1/4 teaspoon black pepper
4 cups oil, for deep-frying
5 tablespoons butter or margarine
2 teaspoons white vinegar
1/4 cup hot sauce, such as Tabasco
1 cup blue cheese dressing

1. Rinse chicken wings under cold, running water and pat dry with paper towels. Sprinkle with black pepper.

2. Pour oil into a wok and heat to 360°F.

3. While waiting for oil to heat, bring butter or margarine, vinegar, and hot sauce to a boil in a small saucepan. Keep warm on low heat until needed.

4. Deep-fry chicken wings until browned and cooked through. Remove wings and drain on paper towels.

5. Brush with hot sauce. Serve with blue cheese dressing for dipping.

Turkey Cutlets with Pineapple Glaze

▶ SERVES 4

5 tablespoons olive oil, divided
1 onion, peeled and minced
1 (8-ounce) can crushed pineapple, drained
$\frac{1}{3}$ cup pineapple preserves
1 tablespoon finely minced ginger
$\frac{1}{4}$ cup flour
1 teaspoon salt
$\frac{1}{8}$ teaspoon white pepper
8 turkey cutlets

1. In small saucepan, heat 2 tablespoons olive oil over medium-high heat. Add onion; cook and stir for 5–6 minutes, until onion begins to brown around the edges. Stir in pineapple, pineapple preserves, and ginger; bring to a boil. Lower heat to medium-low and simmer while preparing turkey.

2. Meanwhile, combine flour, salt, and pepper on shallow plate. Dip cutlets, one at a time, into flour mixture. Heat 3 tablespoons olive oil in large skillet over medium-high heat. Sauté cutlets, 3 or 4 at a time, for 2–3 minutes on each side, until browned and thoroughly cooked. Place on serving platter and top with pineapple mixture; serve immediately.

Turkey Cutlets with Peach Salsa

▶ SERVES 1

1 (5-ounce) turkey cutlet

$1/8$ teaspoon garlic salt

Freshly ground black pepper, to taste

1 teaspoon all-purpose flour

1 tablespoon olive oil

$1/4$ cup quality chunky salsa

$1/8$ teaspoon red pepper flakes

$1/4$ cup diced fresh peach (about $1/2$" dice)

2 tablespoons chopped fresh cilantro, for garnish

1. Season cutlet with garlic salt and pepper. Sprinkle both sides of cutlet with flour. Heat oil in a small nonstick skillet over medium-high heat. Sauté cutlet until lightly browned, about 4 minutes per side. Transfer cutlet to a plate and set aside.

2. Add salsa, red pepper flakes, and peaches to the pan. Cook until heated through, about 2 minutes. Add turkey and any juices; lightly simmer until heated through, about 2 more minutes. Taste and adjust seasoning as desired. Serve hot, garnished with fresh cilantro.

Turkey Cutlets with Home-Style Gravy

▶ SERVES 4

4 (5-ounce) turkey cutlets
¼ teaspoon seasoned salt
Freshly ground black pepper, to taste
2 teaspoons dry poultry seasoning, divided
4 tablespoons butter, divided
¼ cup diced yellow onion
¼ cup diced celery
2 tablespoons chopped fresh parsley
2 tablespoons all-purpose flour
1¾ cups chicken stock

1. Season cutlets with salt, pepper, and 1 teaspoon of the poultry seasoning. Melt 2 tablespoons of butter in a large nonstick skillet over medium-high heat. Sauté cutlets until lightly browned, about 4 minutes per side. Transfer cutlets to a plate and set aside.

2. Melt remaining butter in the skillet and add onion, celery, and parsley; sauté until softened, about 2 minutes, stirring frequently. Sprinkle flour over onions and celery, and stir to mix. Add stock and cook until gravy is bubbling and thickened, stirring constantly. Add turkey, along with any accumulated juices, and lightly simmer until heated through, about 3 minutes. Taste and adjust seasoning as desired. Serve hot.

Turkey and Bean Stir-Fry

▶ SERVES 4–6

1 pound boneless, skinless turkey thighs

3 tablespoons flour

1 teaspoon garlic salt

$\frac{1}{8}$ teaspoon white pepper

2 tablespoons olive oil

2 cups frozen green beans, thawed and drained

1 cup frozen soybeans, thawed and drained

1 cup chicken stock

2 tablespoons cornstarch

THAWING FROZEN VEGETABLES

You can thaw frozen vegetables by placing them in a colander and running warm water over until thawed. Or you can use the defrost setting on your microwave oven. You can also let the vegetables stand at room temperature for 1–2 hours, until thawed. Be sure to drain well after thawing so you don't add too much liquid to the recipe.

1. Cut turkey into 1" pieces. On shallow plate, combine flour, garlic salt, and pepper and mix well. Add turkey pieces and toss to coat.

2. In large skillet or wok, heat olive oil over medium-high heat. Add turkey; stir-fry for 4–5 minutes, until browned. Add beans and soybeans; stir-fry for 3–6 minutes longer, until hot. In small bowl, combine chicken stock with cornstarch and mix with wire whisk. Add stock mixture to turkey mixture; cook and stir over medium-high heat, until liquid bubbles and thickens. Serve immediately.

SEAFOOD MAIN DISHES

Olive Oil–Poached Cod

▶ SERVES 4

4 (6-ounce) fresh cod fillets, skins
　removed
2½–3 cups extra-virgin olive oil
1 teaspoon salt
2 tablespoons fresh lemon juice
1 tablespoon grated lemon zest

1. Rinse fillets and pat dry with a paper towel.

2. Choose a pot that will just fit the fillets and fill it with oil. Bring oil to a temperature of 210°F. Adjust heat to keep the temperature at 210°F while poaching fish.

3. Carefully place fillets in the oil and poach 6 minutes or until fish is opaque in color. Carefully remove fish from the oil and place on a plate. Sprinkle fish with salt.

4. Spoon some of the warm oil over fish and then drizzle it with lemon juice. Sprinkle lemon zest over fish and serve immediately.

Crab Burritos

2 (6-ounce) cans crabmeat, drained
1 cup frozen pepper and onion stir-fry mix
1 (10-ounce) container refrigerated four-cheese Alfredo sauce, divided
1½ cups shredded Monterey jack cheese, divided
12 (6") spinach-flavored flour tortillas

1. Preheat oven to 350°F. Drain crabmeat well, pressing with paper towel to absorb excess moisture. Place in medium bowl. Thaw pepper and onion mix in microwave on 30 percent power for 2–3 minutes; drain well and add to crabmeat. Stir in half of the Alfredo sauce and ½ cup Monterey jack cheese.

2. Fill tortillas with 2 tablespoons crabmeat mixture and roll up. Place in 13" × 9" glass baking dish. Top each filled burrito with some Alfredo sauce and sprinkle with remaining Monterey jack cheese. Bake for 10–16 minutes until burritos are hot and cheese is melted. Serve immediately.

Haddock with Rosemary

▶ SERVES 6

1 cup skim milk
$\frac{1}{2}$ teaspoon ground black pepper
2 tablespoons chopped rosemary, divided
$1\frac{1}{2}$ pounds haddock fillet
2 tablespoons extra-virgin olive oil, divided

1. Mix milk, pepper, and 1 tablespoon rosemary in a shallow dish. Place haddock fillet in milk mixture and marinate 8 hours in refrigerator.
2. Preheat oven to 375°F. Grease a medium baking dish with 1 tablespoon oil.
3. Gently remove fish from marinade, drain thoroughly, and place in prepared baking dish. Cover and bake 15–20 minutes until fish is flaky.
4. Remove fish from oven and let it rest 5 minutes. Cut into 6 portions. Drizzle with remaining oil and sprinkle with remaining rosemary.

Honey Mustard Salmon

▶ SERVES 4

$\frac{1}{3}$ cup honey mustard salad dressing
2 tablespoons honey
$\frac{1}{2}$ teaspoon dill seed

2 tablespoons butter, melted
4 (6-ounce) salmon fillets

1. In shallow casserole dish, combine salad dressing, honey, dill seed, and butter and mix well. Add salmon fillets and turn to coat. Cover and let stand at room temperature for 10 minutes.
2. Prepare and preheat broiler. Remove salmon from marinade and place, skin-side down, on broiler pan. Cover and broil, 6" from heat for 8–12 minutes, until salmon is cooked and flakes when tested with a fork, brushing with remaining marinade halfway through cooking time. Discard remaining marinade. Serve immediately.

Shrimp and Rice

▶ SERVES 4

2 tablespoons olive oil

1 onion, finely chopped

1 cup Texmati rice

1½ cups chicken broth

1 (14-ounce) can diced tomatoes with green chilies, undrained

1½ pounds medium raw shrimp, peeled and deveined

½ teaspoon dried oregano leaves

⅛ teaspoon cayenne pepper

1. In large saucepan, heat olive oil over medium heat. Add onion; cook and stir until crisp-tender, about 3–4 minutes. Add rice and stir to coat. Add chicken broth, bring to a boil, then cover, reduce heat, and simmer for 15 minutes.

2. Add tomatoes to rice mixture and bring to a simmer. Add shrimp, oregano, and cayenne pepper, and simmer for 4–6 minutes, until rice is tender and shrimp are pink and curled. Serve immediately.

Shrimp Fettuccine

▶ SERVES 4–6

1 (16-ounce) package fettuccine

3 tablespoons olive oil

1 onion, peeled and finely chopped

1 pound raw medium shrimp, peeled and deveined

1/2 teaspoon salt

1/4 teaspoon lemon pepper

1 1/2 cups heavy cream or low-fat evaporated milk

1 cup grated Parmesan cheese

1. Bring a large pot of water to a boil and cook fettuccine according to package directions.

2. Meanwhile, heat olive oil over medium-high heat in a large saucepan and add onion. Cook and stir for 4–5 minutes, until tender. Sprinkle shrimp with salt and lemon pepper and add to saucepan; cook over medium heat for 4–5 minutes, until shrimp curl and turn pink. Add cream and heat for 2 minutes.

3. When pasta is cooked al dente, drain well and stir into shrimp mixture, tossing gently to combine. Cook over medium heat for 3–4 minutes, until sauce is slightly thickened. Add cheese and stir gently to coat. Serve immediately.

Pepper-Salt Shrimp or Prawns

▶ SERVES 2–4

1–2 cups oil for deep-frying

Whites of 2 large eggs

¼ cup cornstarch

1 pound fresh shrimp or prawns, peeled and deveined

2 tablespoons Szechuan peppercorns mixed with salt (see sidebar)

1. Heat oil in a medium preheated wok to 375°F. While oil is heating, mix egg whites with cornstarch to form a smooth batter.

2. Lightly coat shrimp with Szechuan peppercorn salt. Dip into the batter. Place a few shrimp at a time into the wok. Deep-fry until they turn golden brown (about 3 minutes). Remove and drain on paper towels.

SZECHUAN PEPPERCORN SALT

Szechuan pepper isn't related to black peppercorns; it's sometimes called Chinese coriander, and is an ingredient in the Chinese five-spice powder. To make Szechuan peppercorn salt, stir together 2 tablespoons Szechuan peppercorns with 4 tablespoons kosher or sea salt. Heat in a heavy skillet over low to medium-low heat, shaking the pan continuously, until peppercorns are aromatic (8–10 minutes). Cool, then either blend the mixture in a blender for a few seconds, or crush in a mortar and pestle.

Curried Shrimp

▶ SERVES 4

1½ pounds medium shrimp, peeled and
   deveined
1½ tablespoons curry powder
⅛ teaspoon chili powder
3 tablespoons vegetable oil
¼ cup sliced green onions
½ cup chili sauce
¼ teaspoon seasoned salt
Freshly ground black pepper, to taste

**CHILI SAUCE
ADDITIONS**

There also are a variety of
gourmet chili sauces on the
market. Try several and find
a brand that suits you best.
You'll find it to be a great
recipe addition when you
need to add zip. You can
also add a few drops of hot
sauce if you're a lover of
spicy food.

1. Pat shrimp dry with paper towels and
   transfer to a medium-sized mixing
   bowl. Add curry and chili powder,
   and toss to coat evenly.

2. Heat oil in a large nonstick skillet over medium heat. Shake off excess
   curry and chili powder and add shrimp and cook, stirring often,
   until shrimp starts to turn pink, about 2 minutes. Add green onions
   and stir to mix. Stir in chili sauce. Cook until heated through, about
   3 minutes. Season to taste with salt and pepper. Serve hot.

Shrimp in Black Bean Sauce

▶ SERVES 4

1 pound large shrimp, peeled and deveined

2 teaspoons cornstarch

2 tablespoons vegetable or peanut oil

2 tablespoons Chinese black bean sauce

1 teaspoon minced garlic

2 slices ginger, minced

2 green onions, quartered

$\frac{1}{4}$ cup chicken broth

1. Place shrimp in a bowl and toss with cornstarch.

2. Heat a wok or skillet over medium-high heat until it is nearly smoking. Add oil. When oil is hot, add black bean sauce and garlic. Stir-fry for 30 seconds, mixing the garlic and black bean sauce together.

3. Add shrimp, minced ginger, and green onions. Stir-fry shrimp until they turn pink and the edges begin to curl, about 1 minute, mixing in with the sauce.

4. Add chicken broth and bring to a boil. Serve hot with rice.

Five-Spiced Shrimp

▶ SERVES 4

1 pound jumbo shrimp, peeled and
   deveined

2 tablespoons cornstarch

3 tablespoons vegetable or peanut oil,
   divided

1 teaspoon minced ginger

2 teaspoons chopped red chilies

1 tablespoon five-spice powder

1 green onion, trimmed and cut into
   1" pieces

CLASSIFYING SHRIMP

The seafood industry uses a combination of size and number to classify shrimp. Whether shrimp are classified as medium, large, or jumbo depends on the number of that type of shrimp that is needed to make up 1 pound. A 1-pound bag of jumbo shrimp will contain only 16–20 shrimp, while a 1-pound bag of medium shrimp will hold 35–40 shrimp.

1. Place shrimp in a bowl and dust with cornstarch.

2. Heat a wok or medium skillet over medium-high heat until it is nearly smoking. Add 2 tablespoons oil. When oil is hot, add minced ginger. Stir-fry for 10 seconds.

3. Add shrimp. Stir-fry briefly until they turn pink, about 1 minute. Remove from the pan and drain in a colander or on paper towels.

4. Heat 1 tablespoon oil in wok or skillet. When oil is hot, add chopped chilies and five-spice powder. Stir-fry for 30 seconds.

5. Add shrimp back into the pan. Stir-fry briefly, coating shrimp with five-spice powder. Stir in green onion and transfer to a serving platter. Serve hot.

Spinach-Stuffed Sole

▶ SERVES 4

¼ cup plus 2 tablespoons extra-virgin olive oil, divided
4 green onions, ends trimmed, sliced
1 (1-pound) package frozen spinach, thawed and drained
3 tablespoons chopped fennel fronds or tarragon
1 teaspoon salt, divided
½ teaspoon ground black pepper, divided
4 (6-ounce) sole fillets, skins removed
2 tablespoons plus 1½ teaspoons grated lemon zest, divided
1 teaspoon sweet paprika

1. Preheat oven to 400°F. Line a baking sheet with parchment paper.

2. Heat 2 tablespoons oil in a medium skillet over medium heat 30 seconds. Add green onions and cook 3–4 minutes. Remove green onions from skillet and place in a medium bowl. Cool to room temperature.

3. Add spinach and fennel to green onions and mix well. Season with ½ teaspoon salt and ¼ teaspoon pepper.

4. Rinse fish fillets and pat dry with a paper towel. Rub fish with 2 tablespoons oil and sprinkle with 2 tablespoons lemon zest. Season fillets with remaining salt and pepper and sprinkle with paprika.

5. Divide spinach filling among fillets. Roll up each fillet, starting from the widest end. Use 2 toothpicks to secure each fillet. Place rolled fillets on the baking sheet and drizzle 2 tablespoons oil over them.

6. Bake 15–20 minutes. Remove toothpicks and sprinkle fillets with remaining lemon zest. Serve immediately.

Grilled Tuna

▶ SERVES 6

¼ cup apple juice
¼ cup dry red wine
1 tablespoon olive oil
½ tablespoon honey
¼ cup minced serrano chili pepper
Zest of 1 large lemon
1½ pounds fresh tuna
2 medium anchovies, chopped
1 teaspoon ground black pepper

MENU IDEAS

Any fish dish is delicious served with a salad made from baby spinach. Toss together spinach, sliced water chestnuts, sliced mushrooms, and red bell pepper, and drizzle with some creamy garlic salad dressing. Top it with croutons or Parmesan shavings. Add some ready-to-bake breadsticks and your meal is complete.

1. In a large baking dish, mix together juice, wine, oil, honey, serrano pepper, and lemon zest. Add tuna and turn to coat. Marinate 30 minutes at room temperature.

2. Preheat a gas or charcoal grill to medium-high heat.

3. Remove tuna from marinade and place on grill. Reserve marinade. Grill tuna 2–4 minutes per side.

4. While tuna cooks, place reserved marinade in a small saucepan over medium heat and cook 5 minutes or until liquid is slightly thickened.

5. Place tuna on a serving platter and drizzle with marinade syrup, then sprinkle with anchovies and black pepper.

Pan-Seared Sea Scallops

> SERVES 4

4 tablespoons butter, divided
1¼ pounds large sea scallops, abductor muscle removed, rinsed and
    patted dry with paper towels
¼ teaspoon salt
Freshly ground black pepper, to taste
¼ cup chopped shallots
½ cup chicken stock
2 tablespoons freshly squeezed lemon juice
1 teaspoon lemon zest
1 tablespoon chopped fresh parsley

1. Melt 3 tablespoons of butter in a large nonstick skillet over medium-high heat. Season scallops with salt and pepper and cook until seared, about 3–4 minutes per side. Transfer scallops to a plate and tent with tinfoil to keep warm.

2. Add remaining tablespoon of butter to the pan. Add shallots and cook until soft, about 4 minutes, stirring frequently. Add stock and lemon juice and bring to a simmer. Cook until slightly reduced, about 4 minutes.

3. Add lemon zest and parsley and simmer for about 1 minute. Taste and adjust seasoning as desired. Transfer scallops to serving plates and drizzle with pan sauce. Serve hot.

Baked Fish Fillets

▶ SERVES 4

1 tablespoon soy sauce
1 tablespoon lemon juice
2 teaspoons bottled minced ginger
Ground black pepper, to taste
½ teaspoon Asian chili sauce, or to taste
1 teaspoon salt
1 pound fish fillets, fresh
½ pound broccoli florets
10 baby carrots, cut in half

SELECTING FRESH FISH

When choosing fish fillets, look for a clean smell and a firm texture, without any discoloration or brown spots. Avoid fish that have a strong fishy smell or yield to gentle pressure. When selecting whole fish, check for bright eyes and a shiny skin.

1. Preheat oven to 375°F.

2. In a small bowl, stir together soy sauce, lemon juice, ginger, pepper, and chili sauce. Rub the salt over the fish fillets to season.

3. Cut 4 sheets of tinfoil, each at least 12" square. Place each fish fillet in the middle of a sheet of tinfoil and brush fillet with a portion of lemon juice mixture. Place ¼ of broccoli and carrots around the fish.

4. Fold tinfoil over fish and vegetables, crimping the edges to seal. Continue with remainder of fish fillets.

5. Bake at 375°F for 15–20 minutes, until fish is cooked through and flakes easily (be careful not to overcook fish). Serve immediately.

Beer-Battered Fish

▶ SERVES 4

¾ cup all-purpose flour
¾ cup cornstarch
1 teaspoon baking powder
1¼ teaspoons salt, divided
1–1½ cups cold dark beer
4 (6-ounce) haddock or cod fillets, skins removed and cut into
   3–4 pieces each
Sunflower oil for frying

1. In a large bowl, combine flour, cornstarch, baking powder, and ½ teaspoon salt. Slowly stir in beer to reach the consistency of a thin pancake batter (you might not need all the beer). Refrigerate batter 1 hour.

2. Rinse fish and pat dry with a paper towel. Season with ½ teaspoon salt.

3. Fill a deep frying pan with 3" oil. Over medium-high heat, bring oil temperature to 365°F. Adjust heat to keep the temperature at 365°F while frying. Fry fish in batches 3–4 minutes or until just golden. Transfer fish to a tray lined with paper towels to soak up excess oil.

4. Season fish with remaining salt and serve immediately.

Fish Creole

 SERVES 6

1/2 cup chili sauce

1 1/2 cups tomato sauce

2 cups medium cooked shrimp

2 tablespoons olive oil

6 (4- to 6-ounce) mild white fish fillets

1/2 teaspoon salt

1/8 teaspoon red pepper flakes

2 tablespoons lemon juice

1. Preheat oven to 450°F. In medium saucepan, combine chili sauce and tomato sauce; bring to a boil over medium-high heat. Reduce heat to medium and simmer for 5 minutes, stirring frequently. Stir in shrimp, cover, and remove from heat.

2. Meanwhile, place oil in glass baking dish. Arrange fish in dish and sprinkle with salt, red pepper flakes, and lemon juice. Bake for 8–10 minutes or until fish flakes easily when tested with a fork. Place on serving dish and top with shrimp sauce. Serve immediately.

Fish Stick Casserole

▶ SERVES 2

1 cup frozen peas

2 cups leftover pasta with sauce

12 fish sticks

1 (10-ounce) can cream of mushroom soup

1. Preheat oven to 425°F. Grease an 8" × 8" baking dish.

2. Place frozen peas in a microwave-safe bowl. Cover with microwave-safe plastic wrap, leaving one corner open to vent steam. Microwave peas on high heat for 2 minutes, and then for 30 seconds at a time, until cooked (total cooking time should be 2–3 minutes).

3. Spread 1 cup of leftover pasta with sauce over the bottom of the baking dish. Carefully arrange fish sticks on top. Stir together soup and microwaved peas. Spoon over fish sticks.

4. Spread remaining cup of leftover pasta on top. Bake for 30 minutes, or until fish sticks are fully cooked. Serve hot.

Easy Jambalaya

▶ SERVES 4

1 (8-ounce) package yellow rice mix

2 tablespoons olive oil

1 onion, peeled and chopped

1 (14-ounce) can diced tomatoes with green chilies

1 (8-ounce) package frozen cooked shrimp, thawed

2 Grilled Polish Sausages, sliced (see recipe in Chapter 7)

FROZEN SHRIMP

You can buy frozen shrimp that has been shelled, deveined, and cooked. To thaw it, place in a colander under cold running water for 4–5 minutes, tossing shrimp occasionally with hands, until thawed. Use the shrimp immediately after thawing.

1. Prepare rice mix as directed on package. Meanwhile, in large saucepan, heat olive oil over medium heat. Add onion; cook and stir for 4–5 minutes, until tender. Add tomatoes, shrimp, and sliced sausages; bring to a simmer, and cook for 2–3 minutes.

2. When rice is cooked, add to saucepan; cook and stir for 3–4 minutes, until blended. Serve immediately.

Garlic Mussels

▶ SERVES 3-4

¹⁄₂ pound spaghetti
4 pounds cleaned mussels
¹⁄₄ cup olive oil
6 cloves garlic, peeled and minced
1 red bell pepper, cut into strips
¹⁄₂ teaspoon dried oregano
1¹⁄₂ cups dry white wine
Salt and pepper to taste

ABOUT MUSSELS

Mussels used to be difficult to prepare because they needed to be cleaned, debearded, and scrubbed. Now you can buy them precleaned, with the beards off; just rinse and use. Be sure to discard open mussels and those with broken shells before cooking, and discard mussels that aren't open after cooking.

1. Bring a large pot of water to a boil; cook spaghetti according to package directions. Meanwhile, place mussels in a colander and pick over them to remove any opened mussels; rinse well and set aside.

2. In large stockpot big enough to hold the mussels, heat olive oil over medium-high heat. Add garlic; cook and stir until fragrant, 1–2 minutes. Add red bell pepper; cook and stir for 3–4 minutes, until crisp-tender. Sprinkle with oregano and pour wine into pot; bring to a boil. Add salt and pepper, then add mussels.

3. Cover pot and turn heat to medium-low. Cook, shaking pan frequently, for 4–7 minutes or until all mussels open. (Discard any mussels that do not open.) Remove mussels and bell peppers from pot and place in serving bowl. Strain liquid and pour half over mussels. Combine remaining liquid with cooked and drained spaghetti; serve immediately with the mussels.

Seafood Au Gratin

SERVES 4

4 tablespoons unsalted butter
3 tablespoons flour
$\frac{1}{2}$ teaspoon dried dill weed
$\frac{3}{4}$ cup milk
$\frac{1}{4}$ cup heavy cream or whipping cream
$\frac{1}{2}$ teaspoon ground nutmeg, or to taste
$\frac{1}{8}$ teaspoon ground black or white pepper, or to taste
1 teaspoon lemon juice
1 pound fish fillets
1 teaspoon salt
$\frac{1}{2}$ cup grated Cheddar cheese

1. Preheat oven to 375°F. Spray an 8" × 8" baking dish with nonstick cooking spray.

2. In a small saucepan, melt butter on low heat. Add flour and blend it into melted butter, stirring continually until it thickens and forms a roux (3–5 minutes). Stir in the dill weed.

3. Increase heat to medium. Slowly add milk and cream, whisking until the mixture has thickened. Stir in nutmeg, pepper, and lemon juice.

4. Rub salt over the fish to season. Lay fish fillets out in the baking dish.

5. Pour white sauce over the fish. Sprinkle cheese on top.

6. Bake fish for 25 minutes, or until it is cooked through. Serve immediately.

HEALTHY VEGETARIAN, VEGAN, AND GLUTEN-FREE MAIN DISHES

Cheese Omelet ◗

▶ SERVES 3–4

1 tablespoon olive oil

3 tablespoons butter

8 large eggs

$\frac{1}{3}$ cup heavy cream

2 teaspoons chopped freeze-dried
  chives

Salt and pepper to taste

$1\frac{1}{4}$ cups shredded fontina cheese

$\frac{1}{4}$ cup grated Parmesan cheese

CREAM OR WATER?

Believe it or not, a battle is raging over whether to add cream, milk, or water to eggs when making an omelet or scrambled eggs. Cream makes the eggs soft and fluffy; water makes the eggs fluffy but doesn't add any fat, so the eggs are not as creamy. All three additions work well; it's your choice.

1. Heat olive oil and butter in a large nonstick skillet over medium heat. Meanwhile, beat eggs, cream, chives, salt, and pepper in large bowl until foamy. Add eggs to skillet and cook over medium heat for 5–8 minutes, lifting edges of the omelet as it cooks to allow uncooked egg mixture to flow underneath.

2. When egg is cooked but still glossy, sprinkle cheeses on top. Cover and let stand for 2–3 minutes off the heat. Uncover pan and fold omelet out onto heated serving plate. Serve immediately.

Tomatoes and Pierogi ◗

▶ SERVES 4

1 cup vegetable broth
$\frac{1}{2}$ teaspoon dried thyme leaves
1 (16-ounce) package frozen pierogies
2 cups frozen baby peas
3 tomatoes, cut into wedges

In heavy saucepan, combine vegetable broth and thyme. Bring to a boil over high heat. Add pierogies, bring to a simmer, lower heat to medium, and cover. Simmer for 5–7 minutes, until pierogies are almost hot. Add baby peas and tomatoes, cover, bring to a simmer, and cook for 3–5 minutes longer, or until pierogies are heated through and vegetables are hot. Serve immediately.

PIEROGIES

Pierogies are large pasta half rounds that are stuffed with mashed potatoes and seasonings, usually onion and cheese. They are a Polish or Hungarian specialty that are sold individually frozen. They cook in only a few minutes and can be dressed with any pasta sauce.

Black Bean Burritos

▶ SERVES 4

1 tablespoon oil

1 cup chopped onion

4 large (12") flour or whole-wheat tortillas

1 cup shredded Cheddar or Monterey jack cheese

2 cups cooked brown or white rice, hot

1 (15-ounce) can black beans, heated with some cumin and garlic

½ cup salsa

1 medium ripe Hass avocado, peeled and sliced

½ cup fresh cilantro sprigs

EAT MORE BEANS

There are more varieties of legumes than it's possible to list here. They are delicious and loaded with protein, vitamins, minerals, and fiber. If you need to stretch your food supply, beans are the answer. They come in red and pink, green and orange, black and white, speckled or solid. Some have black eyes and others look like cranberries. Beans—legumes—are available in many sizes and shapes, from tiny peas to big kidneys.

1. In a medium skillet, brown onions in the oil until soft.

2. Soften a tortilla over a gas burner or in a hot oven; place on a clean work surface. Spoon a quarter of the hot onions into a line, one-third the way up on the tortilla; sprinkle on a quarter of the shredded cheese. Immediately spoon ½ cup hot rice on top; this should be hot enough to melt the cheese. Ladle on a quarter of the beans, including some of its liquid; top with salsa, avocado slices, and cilantro.

3. Fold edge nearest to you up to cover the fillings. Fold side flaps in, to seal ingredients into a pocket. Roll the burrito away from yourself, keeping even tension, and tucking with your fingers as you roll. Repeat with remaining tortillas.

Mushroom Risotto ❧

3 tablespoons olive oil

1½ cups assorted fresh mushrooms, sliced

½ teaspoon dried thyme leaves

1 cup Arborio rice

4 cups vegetable stock

1 cup grated Parmesan cheese

2 tablespoons butter

FRESH MUSHROOMS

The variety of fresh mushrooms is staggering. In the regular grocery store, you can find portobello, cremini, button, chanterelle, shiitake, and porcini mushrooms. Use a combination for a rich, deep, earthy flavor in just about any recipe. Just brush them with a damp towel to clean, then slice and cook.

1. Place olive oil in large saucepan over medium heat. When hot, add mushrooms and thyme. Cook and stir until mushrooms give up their liquid and the liquid evaporates, about 6–8 minutes. Then stir in rice; cook and stir for 3–4 minutes, until rice is opaque.

2. Meanwhile, heat vegetable stock in another saucepan; keep over low heat while making risotto. Add the stock to rice mixture about 1 cup at a time, stirring until the liquid is absorbed.

3. When all the stock is added and rice is tender, remove from the heat, stir in cheese and butter, cover, and let stand for 5 minutes. Stir and serve immediately.

Pesto Pasta

SERVES 4

1 pound linguine
2 tomatoes, seeded and chopped
1 (10-ounce) container basil pesto
$\frac{1}{2}$ cup toasted pine nuts
$\frac{1}{2}$ cup grated Parmesan cheese

1. Bring a large pot of water to a boil and cook linguine according to package directions.

2. Meanwhile, in serving bowl, place tomatoes and pesto. When linguine is cooked al dente, drain well and add to serving bowl. Toss gently to coat pasta with sauce. Sprinkle with pine nuts and cheese and serve.

Tortellini in Wine Sauce

SERVES 4

1 (14-ounce) package frozen cheese tortellini
2 tablespoons olive oil
3 cloves garlic, peeled and minced
$\frac{1}{2}$ cup white wine or vegetable broth
2 cups frozen baby peas
$\frac{1}{4}$ teaspoon onion salt
$\frac{1}{4}$ cup chopped flat-leaf parsley

1. Bring a large pot of water to a boil and cook tortellini as directed on package. Meanwhile, in a large saucepan, heat olive oil over medium heat. Add garlic; cook and stir for 2 minutes, until garlic just begins to turn golden. Add wine, peas, and onion salt and bring to a simmer.

2. Drain tortellini and add to saucepan with wine. Cook over low heat for 4–5 minutes, until mixture is hot and slightly thickened. Add parsley, stir, and serve.

Onion Tart ◗

Pie dough, or 1 (9") frozen pie crust

2 tablespoons unsalted butter

3 cups thinly sliced onions

3 teaspoons chopped fresh thyme leaves, or other herb, such as oregano
or tarragon

1 tablespoon flour

$\frac{3}{4}$ cup half-and-half

$\frac{1}{4}$ cup sour cream

2 large eggs, beaten

$\frac{3}{4}$ teaspoon salt

$\frac{1}{2}$ teaspoon freshly ground black pepper

1. Heat oven to 400°F.

2. Roll dough out to a 10" disk, and fit into a 9" tart pan or pie plate, cutting any excess from edges or crimping in an attractive way; prick bottom lightly with a fork in several places. Place a sheet of waxed paper on the pie shell; fill with pie beads or dried beans and "blind bake" until lightly browned, about 15 minutes; cool on a rack. If using a frozen pie crust, follow directions on the package to blind bake.

3. Lower oven to 350°F.

4. Melt butter in a skillet over medium heat. Add onions and thyme; cook slowly until onions are soft and lightly browned, about 15 minutes. Stir in flour and cook 1 minute more.

5. Transfer mixture to a mixing bowl; combine with half-and-half, sour cream, eggs, salt, and pepper. Pour into prepared pie shell; bake in center of oven until filling is set and lightly browned on top, about 35 minutes.

Brunswick Stew ◗

▶ SERVES 4

4 cups vegetable broth
1 (15-ounce) can diced tomatoes
1 (6-ounce) can tomato paste
1 cup okra, sliced
1 cup corn
1 cup frozen lima beans
2 cups seitan, diced
¼ teaspoon dried rosemary
¼ teaspoon dried oregano
2 teaspoons vegan Worcestershire sauce
Salt and pepper, to taste

DEBATE ON ORIGIN

Some claim that Brunswick stew was first served in Brunswick, Georgia, in 1898, while others say it was created in Brunswick County, Virginia, in 1828. Today, Brunswick stew recipe ingredients vary by region.

In a 4-quart slow cooker, add all ingredients. Cover and cook on low heat for 5–6 hours.

Wild Mushrooms in Vegetarian Brown Sauce ◗

▶ SERVES 2

2 tablespoons peanut oil
1 shallot, peeled and finely chopped
1 tablespoon minced ginger
3 cloves garlic, peeled and minced
3 cups sliced assorted mushrooms (shiitake, oyster, cremini, etc.)
1 tablespoon soy sauce
$\frac{1}{2}$ cup vegetable stock
1 teaspoon cornstarch, dissolved in 1 tablespoon water
$\frac{1}{4}$ cup sliced green onions

1. Preheat a wok over medium-high heat. Add oil. Add shallot, ginger, and garlic and stir-fry 30–60 seconds, so that their aromas are released and shallot begins to turn translucent.

2. Add mushrooms and stir to coat. Reduce heat to medium. Continue cooking, stirring frequently, until mushrooms soften and release their liquid.

3. Add soy sauce and stock. Bring to a boil.

4. Stir in cornstarch mixture. Turn off heat once sauce has thickened. Sprinkle with green onions. Serve hot.

Ginger-Lime Tofu 🌿

▶ SERVES 8

2 (14-ounce) packages extra-firm tofu,
    pressed and sliced into fourths
¼ cup minced fresh ginger
¼ cup lime juice
1 medium lime, thinly sliced
1 medium onion, peeled and thinly
    sliced

CRACKED!

Before each use, check your slow cooker for cracks. Even small cracks in the glaze can allow bacteria to grow in the ceramic insert. If there are cracks, replace the insert or the whole slow cooker.

1. Place tofu fillets in a 6- to 7-quart slow cooker. Pour ginger and lime juice over the tofu, then arrange lime and then onion in a single layer over the top.

2. Cook on low for 3–4 hours.

Okra Gumbo 🌿

▶ SERVES 6

1/2 cup vegetable oil

1/2 cup flour

1 medium white onion, peeled and diced

1 medium bell pepper, diced

4 cloves garlic, peeled and minced

4 cups water

2 cups vegetable broth

1 tablespoon vegan Worcestershire sauce

1 (16-ounce) package frozen chopped okra

1 tablespoon Cajun seasoning

1 bay leaf

2 teaspoons salt

2 teaspoons pepper

1 (7-ounce) package Gardein Chick'n Strips, chopped (or other vegetarian chicken substitute)

1/2 cup flat-leaf parsley, chopped

1/2 cup green onions, sliced

1/2 teaspoon gumbo filé powder

6 cups cooked white rice

FILÉ POWDER

Filé (pronounced FEE-lay) powder is made from ground sassafras leaves. It is an essential ingredient for authentic Cajun or Creole gumbo. Used to both thicken and flavor, filé powder is thought to have been first used by the Choctaw Indians from the Louisiana bayou region. It can be found in most well-stocked grocery stores.

1. In a sauté pan, bring oil and flour to medium heat, stirring continuously until the roux achieves a rich brown color, at least 10 minutes.

2. In a 4-quart slow cooker, add roux and all remaining ingredients except the rice. Cover and cook on low heat for 6 hours.

3. Once done, remove bay leaf. Pour each serving over 1 cup of cooked rice.

Tofu Cacciatore 🌿

▶ SERVES 3

16 ounces soft tofu
1½ tablespoons olive oil
1 shallot, peeled and chopped
4 ounces vegetarian bacon substitute
   (such as Smart Bacon)
1 tomato, thinly sliced
½ cup canned mushrooms
⅓ cup vegetarian chicken-flavored broth
2 tablespoons tomato sauce
1 tablespoon chopped fresh basil
1 teaspoon chopped fresh thyme
½ teaspoon salt

> **REPLACING MEAT WITH TOFU**
>
> Protein-rich and low in calories, tofu makes a great substitute for meat in vegetarian cooking. Always be sure to drain the tofu ahead of time so that it can fully absorb the spices and other flavors in a dish. Also, to make up for the lack of the soluble fat in meat that disperses flavor, consider marinating the tofu in a flavorful marinade before cooking.

1. Remove excess water from the tofu. Cut into 1" cubes.

2. Heat olive oil in a large skillet over medium heat. Add shallot and bacon substitute. Cook for 2 minutes; then add tofu. Cook, stirring tofu cubes gently, for 1–2 minutes, until tofu cubes are browned and shallot is softened.

3. Push tofu to the sides of the pan and add tomato in the middle, pressing down so that it releases its juices. Stir in canned mushrooms.

4. Add vegetarian chicken-flavored broth and tomato sauce. Bring to a boil.

5. Stir in fresh basil and thyme. Stir in the salt. Cook for another minute, stirring to combine the ingredients. Serve hot.

Tofu Salad

▶ SERVES 6

5 tofu cakes, cut into 1" cubes

Marinade:

2 tablespoons water

Ground black pepper, to taste

2 teaspoons sugar

¼ cup dry sherry or Chinese cooking wine

¼ cup soy sauce

¼ cup white wine vinegar

1 clove garlic, peeled and chopped

Pinch of anise seed, toasted and ground

1 tablespoon sesame oil

1 tablespoon vegetable oil

Salad:

1 medium carrot, scraped and julienned

¼ pound snow peas, julienned

1 cup finely chopped cabbage

5 cremini or white mushrooms, sliced

4 green onions, julienned

Dressing:

½ teaspoon salt

2 teaspoons sesame oil

2 teaspoons tamari soy sauce

Juice of ½ medium lemon

Ground black pepper, to taste

1 tablespoon sugar

1. Spread tofu into a single layer in a baking dish or sheet pan. Whisk together the ingredients for the marinade, and pour it over the tofu. Marinate for 3 hours or overnight in the refrigerator, turning occasionally.

2. Combine salad ingredients, toss with dressing, and place in the refrigerator to marinate 1 hour. Add tofu and toss gently to combine just before serving.

Tofu Ranchero 🌿

3 tablespoons olive oil

1 (16-ounce) package firm tofu, drained and crumbled

½ medium onion, peeled and diced

2 cloves garlic, peeled and minced

Juice of 1 large lemon

½ teaspoon turmeric

1 teaspoon salt

¼ teaspoon ground black pepper

1 cup pinto beans, drained

8 corn tortillas

½ cup shredded vegan Cheddar cheese

½ cup chipotle salsa

CHOOSING SALSA

Salsa comes in many delicious and unique varieties. Most are clearly labeled mild, medium, or hot, but one's interpretation of those words can vary greatly. Chipotle salsa has a deep, earthy spice, but you can also use plain tomato salsa or tomatillo salsa in this recipe.

1. Add olive oil, tofu, onion, garlic, lemon juice, turmeric, salt, black pepper, and pinto beans to a 4-quart slow cooker. Cover and cook on medium heat for 4 hours.

2. When ranchero filling is nearly done, brown tortillas on both sides using a small sauté pan.

3. Preheat the oven to 350°F.

4. Place tortillas on a baking sheet and add filling. Sprinkle cheese over the rancheros and bake until cheese has melted, about 5 minutes. Top with chipotle salsa.

Tabbouleh 🌿

1 cup cracked (bulgur) wheat
1 small cucumber, peeled and chopped
3 green onions, finely chopped
2 medium tomatoes, seeded and
    chopped
2 tablespoons chopped chives
1 cup chopped Italian parsley
½ cup extra-virgin olive oil
Juice of 2 medium lemons (about ½ cup)
Salt and ground black pepper, to taste

OLIVE OIL

Spain is the largest exporter of high-quality olive oil, but the United States imports mostly Italian oil. Most (over half) of Italian production comes from the regions of Puglia, Calabria, and Sicily, but in the United States, the only region most people know is Tuscany, which accounts for only a tiny fraction of Italy's extra-virgin exports.

1. Soak wheat in 1 quart of water for 15 minutes (or overnight). Drain and squeeze out excess moisture by tying up in a cheesecloth or clean kitchen towel.

2. Combine with cucumber, green onions, tomatoes, chives, and parsley in a large mixing bowl. Dress with olive oil, lemon juice, salt, and pepper.

3. Set aside to marinate for 2–3 hours before serving.

Chili Bean Dip with Dipping Vegetables

> MAKES 1 QUART

$^1/_2$ pound ground beef

1 onion, peeled and chopped

2 jalapeño peppers (or to taste), cored, seeded, and chopped

2 cloves garlic, peeled and chopped

2 tablespoons vegetable oil

4 teaspoons chili powder, or to taste

1 (13-ounce) can crushed tomatoes with juice

1 (13-ounce) can red kidney beans

$^1/_2$ cup gluten-free beer, such as Redbridge, Bard's Tale, or New Grist (you can leave this out if gluten-free beer is not available in your area)

Assortment of carrots, celery pieces, radishes, broccoli, spears of zucchini, etc.

CHILI AND BEANS

There are endless variations of the chili-and-bean combination. Some people use turkey; others add dark chocolate and cinnamon and vary the amounts of beans and tomatoes. Some forms of chili don't have any beans. Different regions use various amounts of spice, heat, and ingredients.

1. In a large frying pan over medium heat, sauté beef and vegetables in the oil, breaking up with a spoon to avoid clumping.

2. When vegetables are soft, add rest of ingredients (except vegetables for dipping). Cover and simmer for 1 hour.

3. Serve warm, or let it cool and turn this into a dip by pulsing it briefly in the food processor. Do not make it smooth. Serve alongside veggies.

Tuscan Bean, Tomato, and Parmesan Casserole

SERVES 4-6

4 slices bacon

¼ cup olive oil

4 cloves garlic, peeled and coarsely chopped

1 medium onion, peeled and coarsely chopped

½ fresh fennel bulb, coarsely chopped, or thinly sliced green cabbage

1 tablespoon brown rice flour

2 (15-ounce) cans white beans, drained and rinsed

16 ounces tomatoes, chopped (canned is fine)

1 medium zucchini, chopped

1 tablespoon chopped fresh basil

1 teaspoon dried oregano

½ cup rinsed and chopped fresh Italian parsley

1 teaspoon red pepper flakes, or to taste

1 teaspoon salt, or to taste

½ cup freshly grated Parmesan cheese

2 tablespoons unsalted butter, cut into small pieces

1. Fry bacon until almost crisp. Drain on paper towels, chop, and set aside. Remove all but 1 teaspoon of bacon fat from frying pan. Add oil, garlic, onion, and fennel or green cabbage. Sauté over low heat for 10 minutes or until softened but not browned.

2. Preheat oven to 350°F. Blend brown rice flour into the mixture and cook for 3 minutes.

3. Add beans, tomatoes, and zucchini. Mix well and pour into a casserole dish. Stir in herbs, red pepper flakes, and salt. Stir in the reserved chopped bacon.

4. Sprinkle Parmesan cheese and butter over the top and bake for 25 minutes or until the cheese is lightly browned.

Thick and Creamy Corn and Lima Bean Casserole

▶ SERVES 4–5

2 tablespoons unsalted butter

½ sweet onion, finely chopped

½ cup minced celery

½ cup minced celery root

¼ cup chopped roasted red pepper

2 tablespoons brown rice flour

½ cup gluten-free chicken broth

1 (10-ounce) package frozen lima beans

1 (10-ounce) package frozen corn kernels

2 large eggs, well beaten

1½ cups whipping cream

1 teaspoon salt

1 teaspoon sweet paprika

1 teaspoon ground black pepper

1 teaspoon ground coriander

½ teaspoon ground allspice

1 cup gluten-free bread crumbs

1 cup grated Cheddar cheese

BETTER THAN CANNED

While some brands of creamed corn are gluten-free, not all are. It's often easier to stick with fresh or frozen corn, making your own cream sauce. It's easy, naturally gluten-free, and tastes so much better than the ones made with soups or mixes.

1. Preheat oven to 350°F. Melt butter in a large, ovenproof casserole dish over low heat. Add onion, celery, celery root, and red pepper; sauté over low heat until soft, about 10 minutes. Mix in brown rice flour and stir, cooking gently for 3 minutes. Add chicken broth, lima beans, and corn. Bring to a boil and then lower the heat to a simmer and cook until lima beans are slightly softened, about 20 minutes.

2. Remove from heat. Mix together eggs and cream; blend quickly into vegetables. Mix in salt and spices. Place in a well-buttered casserole dish or keep in the same ovenproof pan that you've been using. Sprinkle top with bread crumbs and cheese. Bake until golden brown and bubbling, about 20 minutes. Serve hot.

PASTA AND RICE MAIN DISHES

Microwave Lasagna

▶ SERVES 2

$\frac{1}{2}$ pound ground beef
1 cup crushed tomatoes
1$\frac{1}{2}$ cups marinara sauce
1$\frac{1}{2}$ cups grated mozzarella cheese
1$\frac{1}{2}$ cups ricotta cheese
12 oven-ready lasagna noodles

1. Crumble ground beef into a microwave-safe bowl. Microwave beef on high heat for 5 minutes. Give dish $\frac{1}{4}$ turn and microwave on high heat for 4 more minutes. Make another $\frac{1}{4}$ turn and microwave for 1 minute at a time until beef is cooked through. Remove from microwave and drain fat.

2. Combine ground beef with crushed tomatoes and marinara sauce. Stir in cheeses.

3. Lay out 4 lasagna noodles in a large bowl or a 1-quart microwave-safe casserole dish. (Break noodles if needed to fit into the container.) Spoon $\frac{1}{3}$ of sauce mixture over noodles, spreading evenly. Add 2 more layers of noodles and sauce.

4. Cover dish with wax paper. Microwave on high heat for 7–8 minutes, until cheeses are cooked. Let lasagna stand for 10 minutes before serving.

Linguine with Asparagus, Parmesan, and Cream

▶ SERVES 6

1 bunch asparagus (preferably chubby-stemmed)
2 teaspoons olive oil
2 medium shallots, peeled and thinly sliced
$\frac{1}{4}$ cup white wine
$\frac{1}{4}$ cup vegetable stock or water
2 cups heavy cream
8 ounces linguine, cooked al dente, drained, tossed with a drop of
  olive oil
$\frac{1}{4}$ cup Parmigiano-Reggiano cheese or other top-quality Parmesan
Juice of 1 medium lemon, plus 6 lemon wedges
Kosher salt and freshly ground black pepper, to taste

1. Trim bottoms of asparagus and use a vegetable peeler to peel off the skin from bottom half of stalks. Cut asparagus into bite-sized (about 1") pieces. Heat oil in a large skillet over medium heat; add shallots and cook 3 minutes to soften them. Add asparagus and wine; cook until wine is mostly evaporated, then add stock (or water).

2. When asparagus are mostly cooked and stock is mostly steamed out, stir in cream and bring to a boil; add linguine. Cook until linguine is hot and sauce is slightly thick; add Parmigiano and remove from heat.

3. Season with lemon juice, salt, and pepper. If necessary, adjust consistency with additional stock or water. Serve with lemon wedges on the side.

Linguine Carbonara

▶ SERVES 6

1 tablespoon salt

1 pound linguine

4 large egg yolks

2 teaspoons ground black pepper

1 cup grated Romano cheese, divided

¾ cup diced bacon or pancetta

3 tablespoons water

¼ cup extra-virgin olive oil

¼ cup diced red onion

2 cloves garlic, peeled and smashed

¼ cup dry white wine

PASTA WATER

Adding a little of the pasta cooking water to the sauce helps the sauce thicken (because of the starches in the water). It also helps the sauce stick to the pasta.

1. Fill a large pot two-thirds with water and place it over medium-high heat. Add salt and bring the water to a boil. Add pasta and cook 6–7 minutes or until al dente (follow the package's cooking times).

2. In a small bowl, whisk egg yolks, pepper, and ¾ cup Romano. Set aside.

3. Add bacon and 3 tablespoons water to a large skillet over medium-high heat. Cook bacon until crispy but not hard. Remove bacon with a slotted spoon and set aside. Discard all but 1 tablespoon bacon fat from the skillet.

4. Add oil to skillet and heat 30 seconds over medium heat. Add onions and garlic and cook 1–2 minutes. Add wine and deglaze the pan for 2 minutes. Remove from heat and stir in reserved bacon.

5. Reserve ¼ cup pasta cooking water and drain pasta. Add pasta, pasta water, and egg mixture to the skillet. The residual heat of the hot pasta and pasta water should cook and bind the egg mixture into a thick and creamy sauce. Serve topped with remaining cheese.

Greek Macaroni and Cheese

$\frac{1}{2}$ pound leftover tubular pasta, cooked

4 tablespoons unsalted butter

3 tablespoons flour

1 teaspoon bottled minced garlic

1 cup whole milk

$\frac{1}{3}$ cup crumbled feta cheese

$\frac{1}{4}$ teaspoon ground nutmeg, or to taste

1 teaspoon dried mint

$\frac{1}{4}$ teaspoon ground black pepper, or to taste

1 teaspoon lemon juice

1. Reheat pasta.

2. Melt butter in medium saucepan on very low heat. Add flour and blend it into melted butter, stirring continually until it thickens and forms a roux. Stir in garlic.

3. Turn heat up to medium-low and slowly add milk and cheese. Stir in ground nutmeg and dried mint. Continue stirring with a whisk until mixture has thickened.

4. Stir in pepper and lemon juice.

5. Toss pasta with sauce and serve immediately.

Mexi Mac 'n' Cheese

▶ SERVES 6

3 cups crushed taco chips, divided
8 ounces elbow macaroni
3 tablespoons butter
3 tablespoons flour
2 cups milk
1 cup hot or mild salsa
2 cups shredded Cheddar cheese
Salt and freshly ground black pepper, to taste
4 ounces habanero cheese, cubed
Jalapeño slices
Flour tortillas for serving

1. Preheat oven to 350°F. Layer 2 cups taco chips on the bottom of a 2-quart heatproof dish.

2. Cook macaroni in lightly salted water until al dente. Drain and set aside.

3. Meanwhile, melt butter and whisk in flour and milk, stirring for a few minutes until mixture begins to thicken and is lump-free. Stir in salsa, Cheddar cheese, salt, and pepper. Combine pasta with cheese sauce and spoon into prepared dish. Top with remaining chips, the habanero cheese, and jalapeño slices.

4. Bake for about 30 minutes or until cheese is melted throughout. Serve with softened flour tortillas.

Pasta Frittata

 SERVES 4

1 handful linguine
8 large eggs, beaten
$^1/_4$ cup heavy cream
$^1/_2$ teaspoon dried Italian seasoning
$^1/_2$ teaspoon garlic salt
$^1/_8$ teaspoon garlic pepper
2 tablespoons olive oil
1 cup chopped mushrooms
1 cup grated Cotija or Parmesan cheese

1. Heat a large stockpot filled with water until boiling. Break linguine in half and add to pot. Cook linguine until almost al dente, about 5–7 minutes; drain well. Meanwhile, in large bowl, beat eggs with cream, Italian seasoning, garlic salt, and garlic pepper.

2. Preheat broiler. Heat olive oil in heavy ovenproof skillet over medium heat. Add mushrooms; cook and stir for 3–4 minutes, until almost tender. Add egg mixture to skillet along with drained pasta; arrange in an even layer. Cook over medium heat for 4–7 minutes, until eggs are almost set, lifting egg mixture occasionally to let uncooked mixture flow to bottom.

3. Sprinkle frittata with cheese and place under broiler for 3–5 minutes, until eggs are cooked and cheese is melted and beginning to brown. Serve immediately.

Greek-Style Rigatoni

▶ SERVES 4

$\frac{1}{3}$ cup extra-virgin olive oil

$\frac{1}{2}$ pound rigatoni, cooked according to package directions and kept warm

$\frac{1}{2}$ pound feta cheese, cubed

$\frac{3}{4}$ cup Kalamata olives, pitted and chopped

10 sun-dried tomatoes, drained and sliced

1 tablespoon dried oregano

1 teaspoon ground black pepper

SERIOUS CHEESE EATERS!

Feta cheese accounts for well over half of the 27.3 kilos of cheese the average Greek consumes in a year. No other nation eats as much cheese, not even the French.

1. Heat oil in large sauté pan over medium heat. Add cooked pasta, feta, olives, and sun-dried tomatoes. Toss mixture to combine and cook 2–3 minutes or until cheese just starts to melt.

2. Season with oregano and pepper. Serve hot.

Rotini with Peanut Sauce

▶ SERVES 4–6

½–¾ pound whole-wheat rotini noodles

4–5 tablespoons trans fat–free peanut butter

2 teaspoons brown sugar

2 cloves garlic, peeled and minced

2 tablespoons canola oil

2 tablespoons reduced-sodium soy sauce

1 tablespoon cider vinegar

1 tablespoon sesame oil

4–5 tablespoons hot water

A REALLY NEAT TWIST ON PASTA

Peanut butter with pasta? Sure! To increase the protein level for this dish, add sliced chicken or cooked shrimp—more protein will always keep you satiated.

1. Bring a large pot of water to a boil. Cook pasta until just soft. Drain and set aside.

2. In a medium bowl, combine peanut butter, brown sugar, garlic, canola oil, soy sauce, cider vinegar, and sesame oil. Blend well.

3. Add hot water and mix until you reach a creamy consistency.

4. Add sauce to pasta. Serve immediately for best flavor.

Shrimp Fettuccine

SERVES 4–6

1 (16-ounce) package fettuccine

3 tablespoons olive oil

1 onion, peeled and finely chopped

1 pound raw medium shrimp, peeled and deveined

$\frac{1}{2}$ teaspoon salt

$\frac{1}{4}$ teaspoon lemon pepper

$1\frac{1}{2}$ cups heavy cream or low-fat evaporated milk

1 cup grated Parmesan cheese

1. Bring a large pot of water to a boil and cook fettuccine according to package directions.

2. Meanwhile, heat olive oil in a large saucepan and add onion. Cook and stir for 4–5 minutes, until tender. Sprinkle shrimp with salt and pepper and add to saucepan; cook over medium heat for 4–5 minutes, until shrimp curl and turn pink. Add cream and heat for 2 minutes.

3. When pasta is cooked al dente, drain well and stir into shrimp mixture, tossing gently to combine. Cook over medium heat for 3–4 minutes, until sauce is slightly thickened. Add cheese and stir gently to coat. Serve immediately.

Spaghetti with Olives, Capers, and Tomatoes

▶ SERVES 8

2 tablespoons olive oil

1 tablespoon chopped garlic

$\frac{1}{2}$ cup assorted olives, such as Picholine, Ligurian, Kalamata, or Niçoise, pitted

1 tablespoon small (nonpareil) capers

Pinch of red pepper flakes

$\frac{1}{2}$ cup roughly chopped Italian parsley

2 cups chopped tomatoes

2 cups tomato sauce

Salt and ground black pepper, to taste

1 pound spaghetti, cooked al dente, drained, rinsed, and tossed with olive oil

SKIP THE OIL IN THE BOIL

Adding oil to the pasta cooking water doesn't do anything but make cleanup harder. Pasta added to oiled water still sticks together. The best way to prevent sticking is to stir the pasta immediately after adding it to a sufficient amount of rapidly boiling water. Stir again after a minute or two to catch any remaining clumps.

1. Heat olive oil and garlic in a large, heavy-bottomed skillet or Dutch oven until it sizzles; add olives, capers, red pepper flakes, and parsley. Cook 2 minutes; add tomatoes. Cook until tomatoes soften into a chunky sauce; add tomato sauce, season with salt and pepper to taste, and bring back to a simmer.

2. Add cooked spaghetti; cook until heated through. Remove from heat and serve immediately.

Shrimp, Macaroni, and Feta

▶ SERVES 12

1 tablespoon plus $\frac{1}{2}$ teaspoon salt,
   divided
$2\frac{1}{2}$ cups elbow macaroni
2 red chili peppers, seeded and chopped
3 cloves garlic (2 whole, 1 minced),
   divided
$\frac{1}{4}$ cup chopped fresh parsley
$1\frac{1}{4}$ cups sliced fresh basil, divided
$\frac{1}{2}$ cup extra-virgin olive oil, divided
$\frac{1}{2}$ teaspoon honey
2 tablespoons fresh lemon juice
$\frac{1}{4}$ cup unsalted butter
1 small red onion, peeled and finely
   chopped
1 cup sliced button mushrooms
1 teaspoon sweet paprika
6 medium ripe plum tomatoes, peeled and puréed
$\frac{1}{4}$ teaspoon ground black pepper
$\frac{1}{4}$ cup dry white wine
1 ounce ouzo
1 cup heavy cream or evaporated milk
1 cup crumbled feta cheese
24 medium shrimp, peeled and deveined
1 cup cubed feta cheese
1 teaspoon dried oregano

> **TOMATOES**
>
> It's hard to imagine Mediterranean cuisine without tomatoes. Their bright flavor and rich color make them a staple ingredient in most dishes. The tomato came to Europe via the explorer Hernán Cortés in the 1500s after he discovered the Aztecs eating them in the New World.

1. Fill a large pot two-thirds with water and place it over medium-high heat. Add 1 tablespoon salt and bring water to a boil. Add pasta and cook 6–7 minutes or until al dente (follow the package's cooking times).

Shrimp, Macaroni, and Feta—continued

2. Preheat broiler. Pulse chilies, whole garlic, parsley, ¼ cup of basil, ¼ cup of oil, honey, lemon juice, and ¼ teaspoon salt in a food processor until ingredients are well incorporated. Set aside.

3. In a large skillet over medium heat, heat remaining oil 30 seconds. Add butter, onions, minced garlic, mushrooms, and paprika. Cook 5 minutes or until onions are soft. Add tomatoes and season with remaining salt and pepper. Simmer 5–7 minutes. Add wine and ouzo and cook until most of the liquid has evaporated.

4. Add cream and crumbled feta and cook 3 minutes or until the sauce thickens. Drain pasta and stir into cream-tomato sauce. Add remaining basil and toss to combine.

5. Pour pasta into a medium baking dish and top with shrimp and cubed feta. Broil 5 minutes or until shrimp turn pink and cheese is melted. Drizzle with reserved parsley-basil sauce and sprinkle with oregano. Let cool 5 minutes before serving.

Spaghetti with Tomato and Basil

▶ SERVES 6

1 tablespoon plus 1½ teaspoons salt, divided

1 pound spaghetti

¼ cup plus 2 tablespoons extra-virgin olive oil, divided

8 cloves garlic, peeled and minced

1 (28-ounce) can whole tomatoes, hand crushed

½ teaspoon ground black pepper

1 cup sliced fresh basil leaves

1 cup grated Romano cheese, divided

AL DENTE

Al dente means "to the tooth" in Italian. It refers to pasta that is cooked but not soft. The cooked pasta should be slightly firm and still hold its shape. Perfectly cooked pasta is the best vehicle for a delicious sauce.

1. Fill a large pot two-thirds with water and place over medium-high heat. Add 1 tablespoon salt and bring water to a boil. Add pasta and cook about 6–7 minutes or until al dente (follow the package's cooking times).

2. In a large skillet over medium heat, heat ¼ cup oil for 30 seconds. Add garlic and cook 2 minutes, or until fragrant. Add tomatoes (including liquid) and increase heat to medium-high. Bring to a boil, then reduce heat to medium-low. Season sauce with remaining salt and pepper and cook 10–12 minutes or until thickened.

3. Reserve ¼ cup pasta cooking water and drain pasta. Add pasta to sauce and stir to combine. If sauce is a little thin or dry, stir in reserved pasta water. Add basil and stir to combine.

4. Add ¾ cup cheese and toss to combine.

5. Serve pasta topped with remaining cheese and a drizzle of remaining oil.

Cannellini and Tortellini

SERVES 4

1 (12-ounce) package fresh tortellini
3 tablespoons olive oil
5 cloves garlic, peeled and minced
1 (9-ounce) package soy "meatballs"
1 (19-ounce) can cannellini beans, drained and rinsed
1 (14½-ounce) can roasted tomatoes
Salt and freshly ground black pepper, to taste

1. Cook tortellini according to package directions, drain, and set aside.

2. Meanwhile, heat oil in a large skillet over medium heat and sauté garlic and the "meatballs" for 4–5 minutes. Add cannellini and tomatoes and continue cooking until mixture is heated through. Season with salt and pepper.

3. Add tortellini, stirring to combine, and serve.

Cold Szechuan Sesame Noodles

SERVES 4

8 ounces egg noodles
1 cucumber, peeled and sliced
½ teaspoon salt
1 tablespoon toasted sesame seeds
Szechuan peanut sauce, to taste

1. Prepare egg noodles according to the instructions on the package. Drain.

2. Toss cucumber with salt, and leave for 15 minutes. Toast sesame seeds in a dry pan until they are just fragrant, about 3 minutes.

3. Allow noodles to cool. When cold, toss with peanut sauce. Sprinkle with sesame seeds. Serve over cucumber slices.

Ziti with Peppers and Marinated Mozzarella

▶ SERVES 4

1 pound fresh mozzarella cheese or smoked fresh mozzarella, cut into $1/2$" cubes

3 tablespoons olive oil, divided

$1/2$ cup mixed chopped fresh herbs, such as parsley, chives, oregano, mint, etc.

Pinch of red pepper flakes

1 teaspoon red or white wine vinegar

Kosher salt and freshly ground black pepper, to taste

1 tablespoon chopped garlic (about 3 cloves)

2 cups sliced onions

3 cups sliced mixed bell peppers

2 cups tomato sauce

8 ounces ziti, cooked al dente

1 tablespoon unsalted butter

$1/4$ cup grated Parmesan cheese

1. Combine the mozzarella, 1 tablespoon of olive oil, the herbs, pepper flakes, vinegar, salt, and pepper. Marinate at room temperature for 30 minutes.

2. Combine remaining oil with chopped garlic. Heat a large skillet over high heat, and bring a pot of water to a boil to reheat the pasta. Add the garlic oil to the pan, sizzle 10 seconds until the garlic turns white, and add the onions and peppers. Cook, stirring occasionally, until the onions are translucent. Add the tomato sauce, and lower heat to a simmer.

3. Dip the pasta in boiling water to reheat; transfer hot pasta to the sauce, allowing some of the pasta water to drip into the sauce and thin it. Season to taste with salt and pepper. Remove from heat.

4. Toss with marinated mozzarella, butter, and Parmesan.

Hot, Sour, and Spicy Rice Noodles

▶ SERVES 4–6

¼ pound rice stick noodles
¼ cup dark soy sauce
1 teaspoon sugar
¼ teaspoon chili oil
¼ teaspoon ground Szechuan peppercorn salt (see sidebar in Chapter 9)
¼ teaspoon chili paste
1 teaspoon black rice vinegar
½ cup water
1½ tablespoons oil for stir-frying
¼ cup chopped onion

1. Soak rice stick noodles in hot water for 15 minutes or until they are softened. Drain thoroughly.

2. Combine dark soy sauce, sugar, chili oil, Szechuan peppercorn-salt mix, chili paste, black rice vinegar, and water. Set aside.

3. Add oil to a preheated wok or medium skillet. When oil is hot, add chopped onion. Stir-fry until soft and translucent.

4. Add rice noodles and stir-fry for 2–3 minutes. Add the sauce in middle of the wok. Mix in with noodles and stir-fry until noodles have absorbed all the sauce.

Ginger Peanut Noodles

▶ SERVES 6

¾ cup smooth peanut butter

1 tablespoon honey

⅓ cup low-sodium soy sauce

¼ cup rice wine vinegar

1½ tablespoons toasted sesame oil

1½ tablespoons sambal chili paste

2 tablespoons minced fresh ginger

1 tablespoon minced garlic

1 teaspoon lime zest

½ tablespoon fresh lime juice

¼ cup water

1 pound Shanghai noodles

2 tablespoons vegetable oil

2 tablespoons minced shallots

½ teaspoon red pepper flakes

2 green onions, trimmed and cut into 1" strips

¼ cup crushed roasted peanuts

1 teaspoon toasted sesame seeds

1. In a blender, combine peanut butter, honey, soy sauce, vinegar, sesame oil, sambal, ginger, garlic, lime zest, and lime juice. Blend until smooth. Add water if sauce is too thick. Set aside.

2. Fill a pot with water and bring to a boil. Add noodles and cook for 1–2 minutes. Drain and reserve ¼ cup of water.

3. In a wok, heat vegetable oil to medium and toss in shallots. Stir-fry shallots for 30 seconds before adding red pepper flakes and cooked noodles. Stir-fry for an additional 30 seconds.

4. Ladle in 2–3 spoonfuls of peanut sauce at a time until noodles have been thoroughly coated. Add 1–2 tablespoons of the starchy water to loosen the sauce. Toss in green onions and stir-fry for an additional 30 seconds. Plate the noodles and top with peanuts and sesame seeds.

Basic Cooked Rice

MAKES 3 CUPS

1½ cups water
1 cup long-grain rice

1. Bring water and rice to a boil in a medium saucepan over medium heat.
2. When water is boiling, partially cover and lower heat to medium-low.
3. Cook for approximately 20 minutes until most of the liquid is absorbed.
4. Cover and cook on low heat for about 3–5 minutes. Remove from heat and let sit, covered, for 5 minutes. Use a fork to fluff the rice before serving.

Baked Rice with Red Peppers

SERVES 6

1 cup long-grain rice
½ cup diced red bell pepper
¼ cup extra-virgin olive oil
2½ cups hot vegetable stock
1 teaspoon salt
¼ teaspoon ground black pepper

1. Preheat oven to 400°F. In a medium casserole dish, combine rice, bell peppers, and oil. Toss to coat rice and peppers in oil.
2. Stir in stock and season with salt and black pepper.
3. Bake, uncovered, 40–45 minutes or until liquid is absorbed by rice. Serve warm.

Easy Italian Rice Pilaf

▶ SERVES 4

1 tablespoon olive oil

2 shallots, peeled and chopped

1 teaspoon bottled minced garlic

1 tablespoon chopped sun-dried tomato strips

1 cup chopped red bell pepper

1 cup drained canned mushrooms

$\frac{1}{4}$ teaspoon cayenne pepper

1 tablespoon balsamic vinegar

$2\frac{1}{4}$ cups reduced-sodium chicken broth

2 cups instant white rice

1. Heat the olive oil in a large skillet on medium heat. Add the shallots, garlic, and sun-dried tomato strips. Sauté for 3–4 minutes, until the shallots are softened.

2. Add chopped bell pepper and mushrooms. Sprinkle cayenne pepper on top. Splash vegetables with balsamic vinegar. Cook until vegetables are softened (total cooking time is about 5 minutes).

3. Add chicken broth. Bring to a boil.

4. Stir in instant rice. Cover and let stand off heat for 5 minutes. Serve hot.

Mexican Fried Rice

▶ SERVES 4

3 tablespoons vegetable oil, divided
½ medium yellow onion, peeled and finely chopped
1 tablespoon jarred chopped jalapeño peppers
1 tomato, diced
1 cup canned corn niblets
3 cups cold cooked rice
½ teaspoon ground cumin
2 green onions, finely sliced
¼ teaspoon salt, or to taste
⅛ teaspoon black pepper, or to taste

1. Heat 1½ tablespoons oil in a nonstick skillet over medium heat. Add the onion. Cook for 4–5 minutes, until the onion is softened.

2. Stir in chopped jalapeño peppers. Stir in tomato. Cook for a minute and stir in canned corn. Remove vegetables from the pan.

3. Heat 1½ tablespoons oil in the pan. Add rice. Cook, stirring, for 1–2 minutes, until heated through. Stir in ground cumin.

4. Return vegetables to the pan. Stir in green onions. Stir to mix everything together. Season with salt and pepper. Serve hot.

Chicken Fried Rice

▶ SERVES 4

2 large eggs

2½ tablespoons oyster sauce, divided

⅛ teaspoon salt

⅛ teaspoon ground black pepper

5–6 tablespoons oil for stir-frying

2 stalks celery, trimmed and diced

½ cup chopped onion

4 cups cold cooked rice

1½ cups cooked boneless chicken, chopped

2 teaspoons thick soy sauce

2 medium green onions, trimmed and minced

FLAVORFUL FRIED RICE

Instead of serving fried rice immediately, try storing it in the refrigerator in a sealed container to use another day. This gives the flavors more time to blend. Just be sure to allow the fried rice to cool completely before storing.

1. In a medium bowl, lightly beat eggs. Stir in 1 tablespoon oyster sauce, salt, and pepper.

2. Add 2 tablespoons oil to a preheated wok or medium skillet. When oil is hot, pour egg mixture into the pan. Cook on medium to medium-high heat, using 2 spatulas to turn over the egg mixture once. Don't scramble. Remove and cut into thin strips. Set aside.

3. Clean out wok, if necessary. Add 1–2 tablespoons oil. When oil is hot, add celery. Stir-fry for 1 minute, then add onion. Stir-fry vegetables until tender. Remove.

4. Add 2 tablespoons oil. When oil is hot, add rice. Stir-fry on medium heat, stirring to separate the grains. Add 1½ tablespoons oyster sauce, and an additional small amount of salt and pepper if desired. Blend in chicken, onion, and celery. Stir in thick soy sauce. To serve, garnish chicken with strips of fried egg and green onions.

Mushroom Fried Rice

▶ SERVES 4

2 large eggs
$\frac{1}{8}$ teaspoon salt
$\frac{1}{8}$ teaspoon ground black pepper
1 tablespoon hoisin sauce
2 teaspoons water
3 tablespoons vegetable or peanut oil, divided
3 cups cooked wild rice
1 tablespoon soy sauce
1 cup sliced portobello mushrooms
$\frac{1}{2}$ cup frozen peas, thawed
2 green onions, trimmed and finely chopped
1 teaspoon sesame oil

1. In a small bowl, lightly beat eggs, stirring in salt and pepper.
2. In a separate small bowl, combine hoisin sauce with water.
3. Heat a wok or medium skillet over medium-high heat until it is nearly smoking. Add 2 tablespoons oil. When oil is hot, add eggs. Stir eggs until they are lightly scrambled. Remove scrambled eggs and clean out the pan.
4. Heat 1 tablespoon oil. When oil is hot, add rice. Stir-fry for 2 minutes, stirring and tossing the rice. Stir in soy sauce.
5. Stir in mushrooms. Stir-fry for 1 minute, then add peas. Stir to mix the rice and vegetables.
6. Stir in scrambled eggs, hoisin sauce mixture, and green onions. Cook for 1 minute to blend the flavors. Remove from heat and stir in sesame oil. Serve hot.

Wild Rice with Apples and Almonds

▶ SERVES 8

$\frac{1}{2}$ cup wild rice

$\frac{1}{2}$ cup slivered almonds

1 tablespoon vegetable oil

1 large onion, peeled and roughly chopped

1 Rome or Golden Delicious apple, peeled, cored, and diced

$\frac{1}{4}$ cup raisins

Salt and freshly ground black pepper, to taste

1 tablespoon olive oil

$\frac{1}{4}$ cup chopped cilantro or parsley

SAVING COOKING LIQUIDS AS "STOCK"

Water and broth from boiled wild rice, simmered beans, blanched vegetables, soaked dry mushrooms, and other cooking processes are free gifts. These no-work byproducts come packed with flavor, nutrients, and body, ready to use in any soup, stew, or dish that calls for "water or stock." Freeze them in portion-sized plastic tubs for use anytime.

1. Boil rice in 2½ quarts salted water until tender, about 40 minutes; drain, saving cooking liquid.

2. Crisp almonds by toasting them in a dry skillet until fragrant.

3. Heat vegetable oil in a large skillet or Dutch oven over medium heat for 1 minute. Add onions; cook until softened, about 5 minutes. Add apples, raisins, and a splash of the rice cooking liquid. Cook 5 minutes more, until apples are translucent.

4. Combine cooked rice, apple mixture, nuts, and salt and pepper. Stir in olive oil and serve garnished with cilantro or parsley.

SANDWICHES AND PIZZA

The Basic Burger

▶ SERVES 4

1¼ pounds ground round beef
½ teaspoon seasoned salt
Freshly ground black pepper, to taste
Vegetable oil

1. Lightly mix ground round with salt and pepper, and form into 4 evenly sized patties. Cook by your choice of the following methods:

2. To grill: Clean grill rack and lightly oil to prevent sticking. Preheat grill to medium-high. Cook for about 5 minutes per side for medium, turning once. Transfer burgers to a plate and tent with tinfoil to keep warm. Let rest for 1–2 minutes to allow the juices to reabsorb. Serve hot. If using an indoor grill, follow manufacturer's directions.

3. To broil: Clean broiler rack and lightly oil to prevent sticking. Set broiler rack 4" from heat source. Preheat broiler to medium-high. Cook for about 5 minutes per side for medium, turning once. Transfer burgers to a plate and tent with tinfoil to keep warm. Let rest for 1–2 minutes to allow the juices to reabsorb. Serve hot.

4. On stovetop: Heat 2 tablespoons oil in a large, nonstick skillet over medium-high heat. Cook for about 5 minutes per side for medium, turning once. Transfer burgers to a plate and tent with tinfoil to keep warm. Let rest for 1–2 minutes to allow the juices to reabsorb. Serve hot.

Bacon Burgers

1¼ pounds ground round beef
¾ teaspoon seasoned salt
⅛ teaspoon freshly ground black pepper
¼ cup crispy bacon crumbles
8 (1-ounce) slices sharp Cheddar cheese

1. Lightly mix ground round with seasoned salt, pepper, and bacon crumbles, and form into 4 evenly sized patties.

2. Clean and oil grill rack and preheat grill to medium-high. Cook the burgers for about 5 minutes on each side for medium. Add 2 slices of cheese per burger during the last 2 minutes of cooking. (For alternate cooking methods, see recipe for The Basic Burger in this chapter.)

3. Transfer the burgers to a plate and tent with tinfoil to keep warm. Let rest for 1–2 minutes to allow the juices to reabsorb. Serve hot.

Blues Burgers

SERVES 4

1¼ pounds ground round beef
½ teaspoon seasoned salt
⅛ teaspoon red pepper flakes

½ cup blue cheese crumbles
¼ cup thinly sliced green onions
2 tablespoons vegetable oil

1. Lightly mix ground round with seasoned salt, pepper flakes, blue cheese crumbles, and green onions, and form into 4 evenly sized patties. Heat oil in a medium-sized nonstick skillet over medium-high heat. Cook for about 5 minutes per side for medium, turning once.

2. Transfer burgers to a plate and tent with tinfoil to keep warm. Let rest for 1–2 minutes to allow the juices to reabsorb. Serve hot.

Pizza Burgers

▶ SERVES 4

1¼ pounds ground round beef
½ teaspoon garlic salt
¼ teaspoon red pepper flakes
½ teaspoon dried Italian seasoning
6 ounces pizza sauce
8 (1-ounce) slices mozzarella cheese

1. Lightly mix ground round with garlic salt, pepper flakes, and Italian seasoning and form into 4 evenly sized patties.

2. Clean and oil grill rack and preheat grill to medium-high. Cook burgers about 5 minutes on each side for medium. During the last 2 minutes of cooking, top each burger with a generous tablespoon of pizza sauce and 2 slices of cheese per burger. (For alternate cooking methods, see recipe for The Basic Burger in this chapter.)

3. Transfer burgers to a plate and tent with tinfoil to keep warm. Let rest for 1–2 minutes to allow the juices to reabsorb. Serve hot.

South of the Border Burgers

▶ SERVES 4

1¼ pounds ground round beef
½ teaspoon garlic salt
¼ teaspoon red pepper flakes
4 (1-ounce) slices pepper jack cheese
1 cup quality salsa
¼ cup canned jalapeño slices
¼ cup chopped fresh cilantro

1. Lightly mix ground round with garlic salt and pepper flakes and form into 4 evenly sized patties.

2. Clean and oil grill rack and preheat grill to medium-high. Cook burgers for about 5 minutes on each side for medium. During the last 2 minutes of cooking, top each burger with a slice of cheese. (For alternate cooking methods, see recipe for The Basic Burger in this chapter.)

3. Transfer burgers to a plate and tent with tinfoil to keep warm. Let rest for 1–2 minutes to allow the juices to reabsorb. Serve hot, topped with salsa, jalapeños, and cilantro leaves.

Wisconsin Burgers

▶ SERVES 4

1¼ pounds ground round beef
½ teaspoon seasoned salt
⅛ teaspoon freshly ground black pepper
¼ cup sauerkraut, rinsed and drained
8 slices Muenster cheese

1. Lightly mix ground round with seasoned salt and pepper, and form into 4 evenly sized patties.

2. Clean and oil grill rack and preheat grill to medium-high. Cook burgers for about 5 minutes on each side for medium. During the last 2 minutes of cooking, top each burger with 1 tablespoon of sauerkraut and 2 slices of cheese per burger. (For alternate cooking methods, see recipe for The Basic Burger in this chapter.)

3. Transfer burgers to a plate and tent with tinfoil to keep warm. Let rest for 1–2 minutes to allow the juices to reabsorb. Serve hot.

Spicy Chicken Burgers

> SERVES 4

1 pound ground chicken

$\frac{1}{4}$ cup finely chopped yellow onion

$\frac{1}{4}$ cup finely chopped red bell pepper

1 teaspoon minced garlic

$\frac{1}{4}$ cup thinly sliced green onions

$\frac{1}{2}$ teaspoon hot pepper sauce

1 teaspoon Worcestershire sauce

Salt, to taste

Freshly ground black pepper, to taste

HOT STUFF ABOUT HOT SAUCE

Tabasco is a trademarked name and product held by the McIlhenny family since the mid-1800s. It is produced in Louisiana and manufactured from tabasco peppers, vinegar, and salt. The peppers are fermented in barrels for three years before being processed for the sauce.

1. Clean and oil broiler rack. Preheat broiler to medium.

2. Combine all ingredients in a medium-sized bowl, mixing lightly. Form into 4 patties. Broil burgers for 4–5 minutes per side until firm through the center and the juices run clear. Transfer to a plate and tent with tinfoil to keep warm. Allow to rest 1–2 minutes before serving.

Barbecued Roast Beef Sandwiches

▶ SERVES 12

2 tablespoons olive oil

1 onion, peeled and chopped

$\frac{1}{2}$ cup steak sauce

1 (8-ounce) can tomato sauce

$1\frac{1}{2}$ pounds thinly sliced cooked deli roast beef

12 sandwich buns, split and toasted

1. In heavy skillet, heat olive oil over medium heat. Add onion and cook, stirring frequently, for 5–6 minutes, until onion is tender. Add steak sauce and tomato sauce and bring to a simmer. Stir in roast beef; simmer for 5–6 minutes, stirring frequently, until sauce thickens slightly and roast beef is heated through.

2. Make sandwiches using roast beef mixture and split and toasted sandwich buns. Serve immediately.

Grilled Meatloaf Sandwiches

▶ SERVES 4

$\frac{1}{2}$ cup tomato sauce

4 slices deli meatloaf

4 slices deli Cheddar cheese

8 slices deli pumpernickel bread

$\frac{1}{4}$ cup butter, softened

Preheat dual-contact indoor grill or large skillet over medium-high heat. Spread tomato sauce onto meatloaf slices. Make sandwiches with coated meatloaf, cheese, and pumpernickel bread. Spread outside of sandwiches with softened butter and cook on grill or skillet, turning once, until bread is hot and crisp and cheese begins to melt, about 4–6 minutes for dual contact grill, and 6–10 minutes for skillet. Serve immediately.

Hot Submarine Sandwiches

▶ SERVES 4–6

1 loaf Italian bread, unsliced
$\frac{1}{3}$ cup honey mustard/mayo combo
$\frac{1}{2}$ pound sliced deli ham
$\frac{1}{2}$ pound sliced deli turkey
$\frac{1}{2}$ pound sliced Muenster cheese

MUSTARD COMBINATIONS

There are many types and varieties of mustard combinations in the grocery store these days. From honey mustard to grainy mustard to mustard and mayonnaise blends, there's a large selection to choose from. Keep a supply on hand for making sandwiches from just about any leftover meat.

1. Preheat oven to 400°F. Slice bread in half horizontally and place, cut-sides up, on work surface. Spread cut surfaces with the honey mustard/mayo combo. Arrange ham, turkey, and Muenster cheese on bottom half of the bread, then top with second half.

2. Wrap entire sandwich in tinfoil. Bake for 20–23 minutes or until sandwich is hot, cheese is melted, and bread is toasted, opening tinfoil for last 5 minutes of baking time to crisp bread. Slice into 4–6 portions and serve.

Grilled Steak Sandwiches

▶ SERVES 4

1 cooked steak
1 cup jarred roasted red peppers, drained
8 slices French bread
2 cups shredded Muenster cheese

1. Cut steak into ¼"-thick pieces against the grain. Slice the red peppers into strips. Place 4 bread slices on work surface and top each with ¼ cup cheese. Arrange one-fourth of the steak strips and red peppers on top of each. Top each with another ¼ cup cheese, then top with remaining bread slices. Spread butter on the outsides of the sandwiches.

2. Grill on a dual-contact grill for 2–4 minutes, until sandwiches are hot and cheese is melted, or cook on a preheated griddle or skillet, turning once, about 5–6 minutes.

Greek Pizza

▶ SERVES 4

1 (10" or 12") Boboli pizza crust
1 cup pizza sauce
½ teaspoon dried oregano
1 cup crumbled feta cheese with garlic and herbs
½ cup sliced black olives
2 cups shredded mozzarella cheese

1. Preheat oven to 400°F. Place pizza crust on a cookie sheet and spread evenly with pizza sauce. Sprinkle with oregano. Arrange feta cheese and olives over sauce and top with mozzarella cheese.

2. Bake for 10–16 minutes or until crust is hot and crisp and cheese is melted and beginning to brown. Serve immediately.

Swiss Cheese and Ham Sandwich

▶ SERVES 1

1½ tablespoons mayonnaise
¼ teaspoon cayenne pepper, or to taste
2 slices rye bread
2 slices processed Swiss cheese
2 teaspoons mustard
1 slice cooked ham
½ medium tomato, thinly sliced

1. In a small bowl, combine mayonnaise and cayenne pepper.
2. Spread mayonnaise on the inside of one slice of bread and place the Swiss cheese on top.
3. Spread mustard on the inside of the other slice of bread and add the sliced ham. Add the sliced tomato. Close up the sandwich.

Asian Beef Rolls

▶ SERVES 6

3 tablespoons hoisin sauce
¼ cup plum sauce
1½ cups coleslaw mix
¼ cup chopped green onion
6 slices cooked deli roast beef

In medium bowl, combine hoisin sauce and plum sauce and mix well. Stir in coleslaw mix and green onion and mix gently. Place roast beef slices on work surface and divide coleslaw mixture among them. Roll up beef slices, enclosing filling. Serve immediately or cover and refrigerate up to 8 hours before serving.

Tuna Melts

▶ SERVES 4

4 pita breads, unsplit
4 slices Swiss cheese
1 avocado
1 (6-ounce) can tuna, drained
$\frac{1}{2}$ cup tartar sauce
$\frac{3}{4}$ cup shredded Swiss cheese, divided
$\frac{1}{2}$ teaspoon dried dill weed

SANDWICH MELTS

Melts are open-faced sandwiches, or sandwiches without a "lid," that are usually grilled, baked, or broiled to heat the filling and melt the cheese. Serve them with a knife and fork, and with a simple fruit salad or green salad for a hearty, quick lunch or dinner.

1. Preheat oven to 400°F. Toast pita breads in oven until crisp, about 5 minutes. Remove from oven and top each one with a slice of Swiss cheese.

2. Peel avocado and mash slightly, leaving some chunks. Spread this on top of the Swiss cheese. In small bowl, combine tuna and tartar sauce with $\frac{1}{4}$ cup shredded Swiss cheese. Spread on top of avocado.

3. Sprinkle sandwiches with remaining shredded Swiss cheese and the dill weed. Bake for 7–11 minutes, until cheese melts.

Bacon Crisp Sandwiches

▶ SERVES 4

8 slices bacon
³⁄₄ cup grated Parmesan cheese, divided
¹⁄₂ teaspoon dried thyme leaves
¹⁄₄ cup mayonnaise
4 hoagie buns, sliced
2 tomatoes, thickly sliced

1. Dip bacon slices in ¹⁄₂ cup Parmesan cheese and press to coat. Place 4 slices of the coated bacon on microwave-safe paper towels in a 12" × 8" microwave-safe baking dish. Cover with another sheet of microwave-safe paper towels. Microwave on high for 3–4 minutes or until bacon is light golden brown. Repeat with remaining bacon slices.

2. Meanwhile, in small bowl, combine thyme, mayonnaise, and remaining ¹⁄₄ cup Parmesan cheese, and spread on cut sides of hoagie buns. Toast in toaster oven or under broiler until cheese mixture bubbles. Make sandwiches with the cooked bacon, tomatoes, and toasted buns and serve immediately.

Muffuletta

1 (12") focaccia flatbread
$\frac{1}{3}$ cup bottled olivada, drained
$\frac{1}{2}$ pound thinly sliced fontina cheese
$\frac{1}{4}$ pound thinly sliced smoked turkey
$\frac{1}{4}$ pound thinly sliced salami

MAKE YOUR OWN OLIVADA

Combine 1 cup mixed olives (Kalamata, green, black, cracked) with ¼ cup olive oil, a few cloves of garlic, some thyme or marjoram, and a bit of pepper in a blender or food processor. Blend or process until olives are chopped. Store, covered, in the refrigerator and use it for sandwich spreads or as an appetizer dip.

1. Cut focaccia in half horizontally to make 2 thin, round pieces. Spread cut side of both pieces with some of the olivada. Layer half of the fontina cheese, a thin layer of olivada, smoked turkey, olivada, salami, olivada, and the rest of the fontina cheese. Place top of focaccia and press sandwich together gently.

2. Cut into wedges and serve immediately, or wrap whole sandwich in plastic wrap and chill for up to 8 hours.

Beef and Blue Wraps

 SERVES 4

3 ounces cream cheese, at room temperature

1 tablespoon mayonnaise

2 ounces blue cheese crumbles

$\frac{1}{4}$ teaspoon seasoned salt

Freshly ground pepper, to taste

2 (8") low-carb tortillas, at room temperature

$\frac{1}{3}$ pound lean deli roast beef, trimmed of visible fat, sliced, and cut into $\frac{1}{2}$" strips

$\frac{1}{4}$ cup diced roasted red pepper

1 cup chopped romaine hearts

1. Mix together cream cheese, mayonnaise, blue cheese, salt, and pepper in a small bowl (or use a food processor to blend until smooth).

2. Place tortillas on a clean work surface. Spread half of the cream cheese mixture on the upper third of each tortilla, about $\frac{1}{2}$" from the edge. Place half of the roast beef on the lower third of each tortilla. Top each with peppers and romaine.

3. Roll up each wrap: Starting from the bottom, fold the tortilla over the filling, compressing slightly to form a firm roll. Press at the top to "seal" the wrap closed with the cream cheese mixture. Cut the sandwich in half and wrap in plastic film. Refrigerate until ready to serve.

California-Style BLT Wraps

▶ SERVES 4

3 ounces cream cheese, at room temperature
2 tablespoons mayonnaise
$\frac{1}{4}$ teaspoon seasoned salt
Freshly ground pepper, to taste
2 (8") low-carb tortillas, at room temperature
6 slices smoked bacon, cooked
$\frac{1}{4}$ cup diced avocado
$\frac{1}{4}$ cup seeded and diced ripe tomato
1 cup chopped romaine hearts

1. Mix together cream cheese, mayonnaise, salt, and pepper in a small bowl (or use a food processor to blend until smooth).

2. Place tortillas on work surface. Spread half of the cream cheese mixture on the upper third of each tortilla, about $\frac{1}{2}$" from the edge. Place half of the bacon on the lower third of each tortilla. Top each with the avocado, tomato, and romaine.

3. Roll up each wrap: Starting from the bottom, fold the tortilla over the filling and roll upward, compressing slightly to form a firm roll. Press at the top to "seal" the wrap closed with the cream cheese mixture. Cut the sandwich in half and wrap in plastic film. Refrigerate until ready to serve.

Thai-Inspired Spicy Beef Lettuce Wraps

▶ SERVES 4

2 tablespoons peanut oil or vegetable oil
1½ pounds lean ground sirloin
¼ cup diced red pepper
¼ cup sliced green onions
¼ cup chopped cilantro, plus extra for garnish
½ cup peanut sauce
Asian chili sauce, to taste
Salt, to taste
12 Boston lettuce leaves
½ cup chopped unsalted peanuts

1. Heat oil in a large nonstick skillet over medium-high heat. Add the sirloin, stirring to break up meat into small pieces. Cook, stirring frequently, until meat starts to brown, about 5 minutes. Use a small ladle to remove and discard excess fat.

2. Add red pepper and stir to incorporate; cook for about 3 minutes. Add green onion, cilantro, peanut sauce, chili sauce, and salt; stir to blend. Cook until heated through, about 3–4 minutes. Taste and adjust seasoning as desired.

3. To serve, arrange lettuce leaves on a serving platter. Spoon beef mixture into the center of each leaf and garnish with peanuts and cilantro.

Spicy Italian Sausage Pizza Wraps

▶ SERVES 2

1 teaspoon olive oil
6 ounces spicy bulk Italian sausage
1/3 cup chopped yellow onion
1 teaspoon dried Italian seasoning
4 ounces pizza sauce
2 (8") low-carb tortillas
1/2 cup shredded mozzarella
1/3 cup shredded Parmesan cheese
Red pepper flakes, to taste

1. Heat oil in a heavy nonstick skillet over medium-high heat. Cook sausage, stirring and breaking up larger pieces, until cooked through, about 6 minutes. Use a slotted spoon to transfer sausage to a bowl.

2. Remove and discard all but 1 tablespoon of fat from the skillet. Cook onion until soft, about 4 minutes, stirring frequently. Add Italian seasoning, pizza sauce, and reserved sausage. Stir to combine and cook until heated through and starting to simmer, about 2 minutes. Taste and adjust seasoning as desired.

3. To serve, place each tortilla in the center of serving plate. Place half of the sausage mixture on each tortilla, spreading it about 1/2" from the edges. Sprinkle cheeses on top and add red pepper flakes to taste. Fold over and serve hot.

English Muffin Pizzas

SERVES 6-8

8 English muffins, split and toasted
1½ cups pizza sauce
1 (6-ounce) jar sliced mushrooms, drained
1 cup pepperoni, sliced
2 cups shredded mozzarella cheese

1. Preheat oven to broil. Place English muffin halves on baking sheet and top each one with pizza sauce. Layer mushrooms and pepperoni over pizza sauce. Sprinkle cheese over pizzas.

2. Broil pizzas, 4"–6" from heat source, for 2–4 minutes or until pizzas are hot and cheese is melted, bubbly, and beginning to brown. Serve immediately.

Spinach Cheese Pizzas

SERVES 6-8

6 bagels, split and toasted
2 tablespoons olive oil
1 onion, peeled and chopped
1 (8-ounce) can pizza sauce
Pinch ground nutmeg
1 cup frozen chopped spinach, thawed
1½ cups shredded mozzarella cheese

1. Preheat broiler. Place bagels on a cookie sheet. In heavy saucepan, heat olive oil over medium heat and add onion; cook and stir for 4–6 minutes, until onion is tender. Add pizza sauce and nutmeg; bring to a simmer.

2. Meanwhile, drain thawed spinach in a colander or strainer, then drain again by pressing between paper towels. Spread bagel halves with pizza sauce mixture and top evenly with spinach. Sprinkle with cheese. Broil 6" from heat for 4–7 minutes, until cheese melts and sandwiches are hot.

Meatball Pizza

▶ SERVES 4

1 (14") prepared pizza crust
1½ cups pizza sauce
½ teaspoon dried oregano
½ teaspoon dry mustard
½ (16-ounce) bag frozen meatballs,
    thawed
1 cup frozen onion and bell pepper stir-
    fry combo
2 cups shredded pizza cheese

PIZZA CHEESE

Pizza cheese is usually a blend of Cheddar, mozzarella, and provolone or Monterey jack cheeses, and sometimes Parmesan or Romano. It's available preshredded in the dairy section of your supermarket. You can substitute Co-Jack cheese for the pizza cheese blend—it is a blend of Colby and Monterey jack cheeses.

1. Preheat oven to 400°F. Place pizza crust on a cookie sheet. In small bowl, combine pizza sauce with oregano and dry mustard and mix well. Spread over pizza crust.

2. Cut meatballs in half, and arrange, cut-side down, on pizza sauce. Sprinkle with onion and bell pepper stir-fry combo, then with pizza cheese. Bake at 400°F for 18–23 minutes or until crust is golden brown and cheese has melted and begins to brown. Serve immediately.

Mini Goat Cheese Pizzas

▶ SERVES 8

1 (17-ounce) package frozen puff pastry
    dough, thawed

3 medium Roma tomatoes, thinly sliced

1 (4-ounce) package fresh goat cheese,
    crumbled

2 tablespoons chopped fresh thyme or
    parsley

1. Heat oven to 400°F.

2. Spread pastry on a lightly floured surface and cut out 8 (4") disks. Place disks on a large ungreased baking sheet. Stack another, matching pan atop the disks, and bake until golden brown, about 15 minutes. The second pan will keep the disks from rising too high.

3. Top each disk with 2–3 slices tomato, ½ ounce goat cheese, and about ½ teaspoon chopped thyme. To serve, warm again in the oven for 1 minute, until the goat cheese attains a slight shimmer; serve hot.

CRUMBLING GOAT CHEESE

Cold from the refrigerator, goat cheese crumbles between the fingers, or by flaking it away with the tines of a fork, into attractive snowy-white nuggets. Chèvre is usually sold in 3- to 4-ounce logs. Push the tines of a fork down into the open end of a log, and pry down, twisting to produce attractive crumbs perfect for sprinkling on salads, garnishing soups, or piling on small rounds of French bread.

Spicy Veggie Pizza

▶ SERVES 4

2 cups marinated deli vegetables

1 (12" or 14") Boboli pizza crust

1 (10-ounce) container garlic and herb cream cheese

1 cup shredded provolone cheese

1/2 cup grated Parmesan cheese

1. Preheat oven to 400°F. Chop marinated vegetables into smaller pieces and place in saucepan with the marinade. Bring to a simmer over medium heat; simmer for 3–4 minutes, until vegetables are tender. Drain thoroughly.

2. Place pizza crust on a cookie sheet and spread with cream cheese. Arrange drained vegetables on top and sprinkle with provolone and Parmesan cheeses. Bake for 15–18 minutes, until crust is hot and crisp and cheese is melted and begins to brown.

MAKE YOUR OWN PIZZA CRUST

Make your own crust by combining 2 cups flour, 1 cup cornmeal, 3 tablespoons oil, 1 package yeast, and 1⅓ cups water in a bowl. Knead thoroughly, let rise, punch down, divide in half, and roll out. Prebake the crust at 400°F for 8–10 minutes, then cool, wrap well, and freeze until ready to use.

Sandwiches and Pizza

DESSERTS

Chocolate Chip Cookies

▶ YIELDS 12 COOKIES

2$\frac{1}{2}$ cups all-purpose flour

1 teaspoon baking soda

1 teaspoon salt

1 cup (2 sticks) unsalted butter, softened

$\frac{3}{4}$ cup sugar

$\frac{3}{4}$ cup (packed) light brown sugar

1 teaspoon vanilla extract

2 large eggs

2 cups (12-ounce package) semisweet chocolate morsels

1. Heat oven to 375°F.

2. In a mixing bowl, whisk together flour, baking soda, and salt.

3. In a separate bowl, cream together butter, sugar, brown sugar, and vanilla using a wooden spoon. Add eggs 1 at a time, mixing until incorporated before adding the next one.

4. Add flour in 3 additions, mixing just enough to incorporate after each addition. Stir in the chocolate chips.

5. Drop the dough in tablespoon-sized drops onto ungreased baking sheets. Bake until golden, about 10 minutes. Cool the pans for a few minutes before transferring the cookies to a wire rack to cool completely.

Layered Brownies

1 (14-ounce) package rich and fudgy brownie mix
⅓ cup sugar
1 large egg
1 (3-ounce) package cream cheese, softened
1 cup semisweet chocolate chips

1. Preheat oven to 375°F. Spray a 9" square pan with baking spray and set aside.

2. Prepare brownie mix as directed on package. Pour half of batter into prepared pan and set aside. In small bowl, combine sugar, egg, and cream cheese and beat until smooth and blended.

3. Top brownie mix in pan with cream cheese mixture, then pour remaining brownie batter over cream cheese mixture; marble with a knife.

4. Bake for 19–22 minutes or until top looks dry and shiny. Remove from oven and immediately sprinkle with the chocolate chips; cover with tinfoil and let stand for a few minutes. Remove tinfoil and let cool completely.

No-Bake Apple Cookies

$\frac{1}{2}$ cup butter

$1\frac{1}{2}$ cups sugar

$\frac{1}{2}$ cup brown sugar

1 cup grated peeled Granny Smith apple

$\frac{1}{2}$ teaspoon cinnamon

3 cups quick-cooking oatmeal

1 cup chopped walnuts

$\frac{1}{2}$ cup powdered sugar

1. In heavy saucepan, melt butter with sugars over medium heat, then stir in apple. Bring to a boil, then stir and boil for 1 minute. Remove from heat and add cinnamon, oatmeal, and walnuts; stir to combine. Let stand for 5 minutes.

2. Place powdered sugar on shallow pan. Drop apple mixture by teaspoons into powdered sugar and roll into balls. Place on waxed paper and let stand until the cookies are firm.

M&M's Cookies

1 (18-ounce) package yellow cake mix

1 cup quick-cooking oats

$\frac{1}{4}$ cup butter, softened

2 large eggs, beaten

$1\frac{1}{2}$ cups plain M&M's candies

Preheat oven to 350°F. In a large bowl, combine all ingredients except candies and beat until blended. Stir in candies, then drop mixture by tablespoons onto parchment-lined cookie sheets. Bake for 12–15 minutes or until cookies are set. Let cool for 5 minutes on cookie sheets, then remove to wire racks to cool completely.

Mint Cookies

$^2/_3$ cup margarine, softened

$^3/_4$ cup sugar

$^1/_3$ cup firmly packed dark brown sugar

1 large egg

1 teaspoon vanilla extract

1 (1-ounce) square unsweetened chocolate, melted

$1^1/_2$ cups all-purpose flour

1 (10-ounce) package mint chocolate morsels

1. Preheat oven to 325°F. In a mixing bowl, beat margarine at medium speed with an electric mixer.

2. Gradually add white and brown sugars. Mix well. Add egg, vanilla extract, and melted chocolate and continue to beat. Gradually add flour until batter is smooth.

3. By hand, stir in mint morsels.

4. Spray nonstick cooking spray on a baking sheet. Drop large teaspoons of dough onto the baking sheet.

5. Bake 10–15 minutes. Cool on a wire rack before serving.

Easy Fudge

1 (12-ounce) package semisweet chocolate chips
1/2 cup milk chocolate chips
1 (15-ounce) can sweetened condensed milk
1 cup chopped cashews
1 cup miniature marshmallows

1. Grease an 8" square pan with butter and set aside. In medium microwave-safe bowl, combine semisweet chocolate chips, milk chocolate chips, and sweetened condensed milk. Microwave on 50 percent power for 2–4 minutes, stirring once during cooking time, until chocolate is almost melted. Remove from microwave and stir until chocolate melts.

2. Stir in cashews until mixed, then stir in marshmallows. Spread into prepared pan and let stand until cool.

Mint Mousse

2 cups vanilla ice cream
2 cups mint chip ice cream
1/4 teaspoon peppermint extract
1/4 cup whipping cream
16 chocolate-mint-layered rectangular candies, coarsely chopped

In blender or food processor, combine vanilla ice cream and mint chip ice cream, peppermint extract, and whipping cream; blend or process until smooth and creamy. Quickly spoon into parfait glasses or custard cups and top with chopped candies. Serve immediately.

Graham Fudge Squares

1 cup sugar
¾ cup flour
½ cup butter
1 (15-ounce) can sweetened condensed milk
2 cups semisweet chocolate chips, divided
1½ cups cinnamon graham cracker crumbs

1. Grease 9" square pan with butter and set aside. In heavy saucepan, mix sugar, flour, butter, and sweetened condensed milk. Bring to a boil over medium-high heat, stirring constantly. Let boil for 1 minute, stirring constantly. Remove from heat and add 1¼ cups of the chocolate chips. Stir until chocolate melts and mixture is smooth.

2. Add graham cracker crumbs and mix well. Spread in prepared pan and press down. In microwave-safe bowl, place remaining ¾ cup chocolate chips. Microwave on medium power (50 percent) for 1 minute. Remove and stir until smooth. Pour over graham cracker mixture and spread to cover. Chill in freezer for 10–15 minutes, then cut into bars to serve.

Chocolate Raspberry Pie

▶ SERVES 8

1 cup semisweet chocolate chips
1 (8-ounce) package cream cheese, softened
1 (9") chocolate cookie pie crust
$\frac{1}{4}$ cup raspberry jelly
2 cups fresh raspberries

1. Put chocolate chips in a small microwave-safe bowl. Microwave at 50 percent power for 1½ minutes; stir until chips are melted. Cut cream cheese into cubes and add to melted chips; beat well until smooth. Place mixture in refrigerator for 10 minutes.

2. Spread cooled chocolate mixture in bottom of pie crust. Put jelly in medium saucepan over low heat; cook and stir just until jelly is almost melted. Remove from heat and gently fold in raspberries just until coated. Place on top of the chocolate mixture. Serve immediately or cover and refrigerate until serving time.

Brownie Parfait

▶ SERVES 8

5 plain brownies
2 cups coffee ice cream
2 cups vanilla ice cream
1 cup chocolate fudge ice cream topping
½ cup English toffee bits

Cut brownies into 1" squares. Stir both flavors of ice cream until slightly softened. Layer brownies, ice cream, and fudge topping in 8 parfait glasses. Sprinkle with toffee bits. Serve immediately or freeze up to 8 hours; if frozen, let stand at room temperature for 10–15 minutes before serving.

PARFAIT GLASSES

Parfait glasses and iced-tea spoons are the perfect utensils to use when making parfaits. The long and slender parfait glasses allow lots of beautiful layers to show through, and the iced-tea spoons are long enough to reach down to the bottom of the glasses.

Apple Crumble

▶ SERVES 6

1 (21-ounce) can apple pie filling
¾ cup brown sugar
1 teaspoon cinnamon
¼ teaspoon nutmeg

½ cup flour
½ cup oatmeal
⅓ cup butter, melted

1. Preheat oven to 400°F. Place pie filling into 1½-quart casserole. In medium bowl, combine sugar, cinnamon, nutmeg, flour, and oatmeal and mix well. Add melted butter and mix until crumbs form. Sprinkle crumbs over pie filling.

2. Bake for 15–20 minutes or until pie filling bubbles and crumb mixture is browned. Serve warm.

Blueberry Crisp

SERVES 6

1 (21-ounce) can blueberry pie filling
$^1\!/_2$ cup flour
$^1\!/_2$ cup brown sugar
$^1\!/_2$ cup oatmeal
$^1\!/_2$ cup chopped walnuts
$^1\!/_2$ teaspoon cinnamon
$^1\!/_4$ cup butter, melted

1. Preheat oven to 400°F. Pour blueberry pie filling into 9" square glass pan and set aside.

2. In medium bowl, combine flour, brown sugar, oatmeal, walnuts, and cinnamon and mix well. Pour butter into flour mixture and stir until mixture is crumbly. Sprinkle over blueberry pie filling. Bake for 20–25 minutes or until filling is bubbly and crust is light golden brown. Serve with ice cream or whipped cream.

CRISPS, CRUMBLES, GRUNTS, AND COBBLERS

All of these old-fashioned, homey desserts are basically the same thing: fruits with some kind of topping. Crisps use oatmeal and nuts to form a crumbly topping; crumbles are the same thing. Grunts are more like a steamed pudding, sometimes cooked on top of the stove. Cobblers are similar to a deep-dish pie, with a thick biscuit-type crust.

Grilled Peaches

SERVES 4

4 peaches, cut in half
3 tablespoons brown sugar
3 tablespoons maple syrup

$^1/_2$ teaspoon cinnamon
$^1/_2$ cup heavy cream

1. Remove pits from peaches. Prepare and preheat grill. In small bowl, combine sugar, syrup, and cinnamon. Brush this mixture over both sides of peaches. Place peaches, cut-side down, 4"–6" from medium coals.

2. Grill, uncovered, for 2–3 minutes, then turn peaches and top with remaining brown sugar mixture. Grill for 1–2 minutes longer, then remove. Drizzle with cream and serve.

Flaky Peach Tarts

SERVES 6

1 sheet frozen puff pastry, thawed
2 peaches
$^1/_3$ cup peach jam
3 tablespoons brown sugar
$^1/_8$ teaspoon cinnamon

TOPPING TARTS

Tarts can be topped with sweetened whipped cream, ice cream, or hard sauce. To make hard sauce, beat $^1/_2$ cup softened butter with 1 cup powdered sugar and 1 teaspoon vanilla. Serve on hot desserts; the mixture will melt into the dessert and form a sweet sauce.

1. Preheat oven to 375°F. Roll pastry into a 9" × 12" rectangle. Cut pastry into 12 (3") squares and place on parchment paper–lined cookie sheets; set aside.

2. Peel peaches, remove pit, and cut into thin slices. Arrange peach slices on pastry and brush each with some of the peach jam. Sprinkle with brown sugar and cinnamon. Bake for 10–14 minutes or until pastry is puffed and golden and fruit is tender.

Marshmallow Treats

▶ YIELDS 12 COOKIES

4 cups miniature marshmallows
$\frac{1}{4}$ cup peanut butter
2 tablespoons butter
4 cups toasted rice flakes cereal
1 cup miniature chocolate chips
12 large marshmallows

1. Combine miniature marshmallows, peanut butter, and butter in large microwave-safe bowl. Microwave on high for 1–3 minutes or until marshmallows are melted, stirring once during cooking time. Stir well to combine. Add rice cereal and miniature chocolate chips and mix well.

2. Form a scant $\frac{1}{4}$ cup cereal mixture around each large marshmallow and form a ball, using greased hands. Refrigerate about 10–15 minutes, until firm. Wrap in cellophane and store at room temperature.

SUBSTITUTIONS

For a nice treat, you can substitute many things for the large marshmallows in these easy cookies. You can use chocolate kisses, either milk chocolate or dark; miniature candy bars; dates; or dried apricots. Or you don't need a filling at all! The cereal mixture can also be pressed into a 13" × 9" pan and cut into bars.

Microwave S'mores

12 whole graham crackers (2-part square)
1 cup semisweet chocolate chips
½ cup mini marshmallows

1. Lay 6 graham crackers in a microwave-safe shallow baking dish.
2. In a small bowl, stir together the chocolate chips and marshmallows.
3. Arrange the chocolate and marshmallows over the graham crackers.
4. Microwave on high heat for 1½ minutes, and then for 15–30 seconds at a time until the chocolate and marshmallows are melted.
5. Remove and top each s'more with a graham cracker to make a sandwich.

Mini Fruit Tarts

24 frozen mini phyllo tart shells
½ cup apple jelly
½ teaspoon chopped fresh thyme leaves
½ cup blueberries
½ cup raspberries

1. Preheat oven to 375°F. Place tart shells on a cookie sheet and bake according to package directions. Remove to wire racks.
2. Meanwhile, heat apple jelly and thyme in a medium saucepan over low heat until jelly melts. Remove from heat and stir in berries. Put a couple of teaspoons of berry mixture into each tart shell and serve.

Strawberries with Sour Cream

 SERVES 6

2 pints strawberries, stemmed and sliced
1 cup sour cream
$\frac{1}{2}$ cup brown sugar
$\frac{1}{4}$ cup toasted pecans

In glass serving bowl, place $\frac{1}{3}$ of the strawberries. Top with $\frac{1}{3}$ of the sour cream and sprinkle with $\frac{1}{3}$ of the brown sugar. Repeat layers, ending with brown sugar. Top with toasted pecans and serve, or cover and refrigerate up to 8 hours.

Strawberry Parfait

 SERVES 4

1 cup strawberries, rinsed, dried, and hulled
$1\frac{1}{2}$ cups nondairy whipped topping (such as Cool Whip), thawed
$\frac{1}{2}$ cup light, sugar-free strawberry preserves
4 whole strawberries
Fresh mint sprigs, for garnish

1. Slice strawberries lengthwise and divide equally between 4 chilled martini glasses or ramekins.
2. Combine whipped topping with preserves in a medium-sized mixing bowl and stir until evenly blended. Dollop mixture on top of the fruit or use a piping bag to top each with a rosette. Garnish each with a whole strawberry and a fresh mint sprig.

Sliced Strawberries with Custard Sauce

▶ SERVES 6

1¼ cups whole milk
1 vanilla bean, split
1 strip orange zest
1 large egg
3 tablespoons sugar or equivalent sugar substitute
1 tablespoon Grand Marnier
3⅓ cups hulled and sliced strawberries
Fresh mint leaves, for garnish

1. Rinse a heavy saucepan with cold water and shake dry to help prevent sticking. Combine milk, vanilla bean, and orange zest in the saucepan over medium heat. Bring to a simmer and remove from heat.

2. Combine egg and sugar in a small mixing bowl and beat until smooth but not fluffy. Temper mixture by slowly mixing a little of the hot milk mixture into the eggs. Add a little more hot milk, mix, add remaining milk, and whisk until combined.

3. Cook over medium heat, stirring constantly with a wooden spoon. Cook until custard is thick enough to coat the back of a wooden spoon, about 8 minutes. Do not boil or sauce will curdle.

4. Strain sauce into a clean bowl set on ice. Discard orange zest. Scrape seeds from the vanilla bean and put seeds back into sauce. Add Grand Marnier and continue to stir until the sauce is chilled. Add more ice if needed to chill quickly.

5. To serve, divide strawberries equally between 6 ramekins. Drizzle custard sauce over berries and top with fresh mint leaves. Serve chilled.

Peanut Butter Cups

▶ SERVES 8

½ cup crunchy peanut butter
1 (8-ounce) package cream cheese (soy or regular), at room temperature
¾ cup packed brown sugar
1 large egg, lightly beaten
3 tablespoons cornstarch
½ cup chocolate morsels
1 (16.3-ounce) tube flaky refrigerator biscuits

1. Preheat oven to 375°F. Spray muffin tins with nonstick cooking spray.

2. Combine peanut butter, cream cheese, and sugar in a mixing bowl and beat until smooth. Add egg and cornstarch and beat again. Fold morsels in by hand.

3. Roll out biscuits one at a time on a lightly floured surface and fit each into a muffin cup so that it forms a "crust." Spoon peanut butter mixture into each biscuit crust. Reduce temperature to 350°F.

4. Bake for 25–30 minutes, or until center feels firm to touch. Remove from oven and cool to firm completely.

APPENDIX:
GLOSSARY OF BASIC COOKING TERMS

baste:

To spoon or brush a liquid over food—usually meat—during cooking. Basting prevents the food from drying out while being cooked. The basting liquid can be anything from a specially prepared sauce to the pan juices from meat that is cooking.

blanch:

To plunge vegetables and other food briefly into boiling water. Blanching seals in the color and textures of tender-crisp vegetables, such as asparagus. It's also a quick and easy way to loosen the skins on nuts, tomatoes, and other fruit, and to remove the salty flavor from foods such as ham. Blanched food that isn't going to be cooked immediately should be plunged in ice-cold water. This "shocks" the food and stops the cooking process.

boil:

To heat a liquid until bubbles form on the surface, or to cook food by placing it in liquid that is boiling. In a "rolling boil" the entire liquid is boiling, not just the surface. Stirring with a spoon won't cause the liquid to stop boiling.

braise:

To cook meat with a small amount of liquid in a tightly covered pan. Usually, the meat is browned before braising. This cooking method is an easy way to tenderize cheaper cuts of meat.

broil:

To cook food right above or under a heat source. Food can be broiled indoors in the oven or outdoors on a grill. When broiling meat, use a rack or broiling pan so that the fat from the meat can drain.

brown:

To briefly fry meat in oil until it is browned on both sides, but not cooked through. Browning the meat helps keep it tender by sealing in its natural juices.

caramelize:
To heat sugar until it becomes golden and has a syrupy texture. Meat can be caramelized by heating it in a frying pan to draw out its natural juices, which brown—or "caramelize"—on the bottom of the pan.

chop:
To cut food into small pieces, not necessarily of a uniform size. Garlic is frequently chopped before frying.

deglaze:
To add liquid to a pan or roasting pan that contains caramelized meat juices. Heating the liquid makes it easier to scrape up the hardened meat juices, which are combined with the liquid to create a sauce.

dice:
To cut food into small cubes no larger than ¼".

drain:
To remove the water from blanched, washed, rinsed, or boiled food. For hassle-free draining, purchase a colander. Depending on your budget, several varieties are available, from stainless steel to inexpensive plastic.

dredge:
To coat food—usually meat or seafood—with a dry ingredient before frying. Depending on the recipe, the dry ingredient can be anything from flour or cornstarch to bread crumbs or cornmeal. Dredging provides a crisp coating and helps seal in flavor. For best results, food should be fried immediately after the coating is applied.

marinate:
To soak food in a liquid before cooking, both to tenderize it and add flavor. Most marinades contain an acidic ingredient such as lemon juice, wine, or vinegar.

mince:
To cut food into very small pieces. Minced food is cut more finely than chopped food.

sauté:
To quickly cook food in a pan in a small amount of oil, butter, or other fat.

simmer:
To cook food in liquid that is almost, but not quite, boiling.

steam:
To cook food in the steam produced by a small amount of boiling water.

METRIC CONVERSION TABLE

VOLUME CONVERSIONS

U.S. Volume Measure	Metric Equivalent
⅛ teaspoon	0.5 milliliter
¼ teaspoon	1 milliliter
½ teaspoon	2 milliliters
1 teaspoon	5 milliliters
½ tablespoon	7 milliliters
1 tablespoon (3 teaspoons)	15 milliliters
2 tablespoons (1 fluid ounce)	30 milliliters
¼ cup (4 tablespoons)	60 milliliters
⅓ cup	90 milliliters
½ cup (4 fluid ounces)	125 milliliters
⅔ cup	160 milliliters
¾ cup (6 fluid ounces)	180 milliliters
1 cup (16 tablespoons)	250 milliliters
1 pint (2 cups)	500 milliliters
1 quart (4 cups)	1 liter (about)

WEIGHT CONVERSIONS

U.S. Weight Measure	Metric Equivalent
½ ounce	15 grams
1 ounce	30 grams
2 ounces	60 grams
3 ounces	85 grams
¼ pound (4 ounces)	115 grams
½ pound (8 ounces)	225 grams
¾ pound (12 ounces)	340 grams
1 pound (16 ounces)	454 grams

INDEX